V-BOMBERS

Modern Combat Aircraft 11
V-BOMBERS
Robert Jackson

LONDON
IAN ALLAN LTD

Contents

First published 1981

ISBN 0 7110 1100 1

Design by Offa Jones LSIAD FRSA

Published by Ian Allan Ltd, Shepperton, Surrey,
and printed by Ian Allan Printing Ltd at their works
at Coombelands in Runnymede, England.

Cover: Vulcan B2s of No 1 Group, RAF Strike Command, on the
flight line at Barksdale AFB, Louisiana, during the SAC Bombing
Competition 'Giant Voice'./*Martin Horseman*

Title page: A Vulcan B2 of RAF Scampton./*MoD*

Preface

To the majority of people who lived through the dangerous 'cold war' years of the late 1950s and early 1960s, the term 'western nuclear deterrent' meant the mightly shield of America's Strategic Air Command, with its arsenal of global-range bombers and missiles. It is often overlooked that, in the event of a nuclear war, the spearhead of the West's manned bomber retaliatory forces would have been provided by the medium bombers of the RAF – the Valiants, Vulcans and Victors of the V-Force.

This is the story of the V-Force, and of the aircraft on which it was based. It is incomplete, for much is still secret – hidden under the cloak of the 'Thirty-Year Rule', which supresses the release of military information for that period of time. It will be the end of the century before the full story of Britain's airborne strategic nuclear deterrent is told.

In preparing this book I have had the assistance of many people, some of whom must, of necessity, remain anonymous. I would, however, like to express thanks to the staff of the Air Historical Branch of the Ministry of Defence, and in particular to Mr Humphrey Wynn, who verified certain information; to John Hardy and John McCauley, for their reminiscences; and to Bill Gunston, who has forgotten more about bombers than I will ever know.

The Origins of the V-Bombers

When World War 2 broke out in September 1939, Great Britain, alone among the major powers, possessed a bomber force that could truly be described as strategic. Such a force had in fact been in existence since the summer of 1918, when a strategic bombing element – known as the Independent Force, RAF – had been formed under the command of Maj-Gen Sir Hugh Trenchard to carry out attacks by day and night against industrial targets in Germany, railway centres and aerodromes. It was the first time that an air force had been formed for the express purpose of conducting a war without reference or subordination to either Army or Navy.

Small though RAF Bomber Command's strategic force was in 1939, it nevertheless provided the anvil on which a mighty sword was forged: the striking force of four-engined heavy bombers which, from the summer of 1942, began to attack Germany's industrial heartland with growing power. In that year, too, the United States entered the strategic bombing war, with the arrival in Britain of the first units of the USAAF 8th Air Force; but for the Americans the strategic bomber was a relatively new concept, their land-based power having been assigned to the role of army support. The same was true of the air arms of both Germany and the USSR, neither of which succeeded in creating a significant strategic bombing force during World War 2.

By the war's end, the United States had taken over the lead in strategic bomber design. Whereas the RAF's requirements had called for a bomber capable of delivering a heavy bomb load over medium ranges, resulting in the Short Stirling, Avro Lancaster and Handley Page Halifax, the USAAF's requirement had been different, mainly because of geographical considerations. In the late 1930s, with Imperial Japan posing an increasing threat to American interests in the Pacific, several US aircraft companies had been asked to submit design studies for a new and advanced bomber capable of carrying a substantial bomb load over great distances; one which, in other words, would be able to strike at Japan from advanced US Pacific bases.

The result was the Boeing B-29 Superfortress, the largest, heaviest and most advanced bomber employed during World War 2. With a normal range of 3,250 miles – twice that of, say, the Lancaster or Boeing's earlier design, the B-17 Flying Fortress – a top speed of 357mph at 30,000ft and a bomb load of 12,000lb, this was the aircraft which, in 1944-45, brought home the war to the Japanese home islands and dropped the world's first operational atomic bombs on Hiroshima and Nagasaki.

It was also the aircraft which enabled the USSR to enter the strategic bomber stakes, for in the closing months of 1944 three B-29s made emergency landings on Soviet territory after attacking Japanese targets and were immediately appropriated by the Russians. A copy, the Tupolev Tu-4, flew in 1946, and deliveries to the squadrons of the Soviet Long-Range Aviation (*Dalnaya Aviatsiya*) began in 1948. This gave the Russians a long-range strategic capability much sooner than if they had been compelled to rely on an indigenous design, which would probably not have flown before 1950, and by that time the Americans had a truly global bomber in service, the giant Convair B-36.

The B-36, however, massive though it was, was conventional in design, and although its six piston engines were later supplemented by four turbojets mounted in pods under the wings it had neither the speed nor the ceiling to evade contemporary jet fighters. In 1950, the bulk of Strategic Air Command's combat wings were still equipped with either the B-29 or its derivative, the B-50, and the first months of the Korean War tragically proved the inability of piston-engined bombers to survive in a hostile environment ruled by jet interceptors.

The answer to the problem clearly lay in coupling the turbojet with an advanced aerodynamic design, and American studies in this area had begun in a tentative fashion as early as 1943. When the USAAF eventually issued a specification for a jet medium bomber, Boeing, Convair, Martin and North American all submitted designs, and it was North American's, the four-jet B-45 Tornado, which was

Top right: The Boeing B-29 Superfortress was the most advanced bomber to be employed during World War 2 and saw the beginning of the USA's strategic bombing fleet. However, it was piston-engined and the air battles over Korea showed up the vulnerability of piston-engined bombers to jet interceptors. *Right:* In 1947 the Boeing XB-47 flew for the first time; entering service in 1951 the B-47 gave the Americans a considerable lead in development of a nuclear-capable bombing fleet.

the first to fly in March 1947 and subsequently to enter service with SAC. However, it was Boeing's design – or rather, the end product of a series of designs – which gave Strategic Air Command, which was formed in 1946, the revolutionary bomber it needed to put it a long way ahead of any competitor.

Its design drawing heavily on wartime German research data on swept wings and their value at high Mach numbers, the Boeing XB-47 Stratojet flew for the first time in December 1947, and the first fully-cleared production version, the B-47B, entered service with SAC in 1951. At a time when the world seemed to be on the brink of a full-scale conflict between East and West, the B-47 gave the Americans a hitherto unparalleled capability to deliver nuclear weapons to the heartland of a potential enemy, and its advent marked the real birth of the free world's nuclear deterrent force.

Such, in broad outline, was the American strategic bomber situation in the United States at the close of World War 2 and in the immediate postwar years. The position in Britain, however, was very different.

Here, the emphasis during the war had been on developing existing bomber designs to their limit, rather than on seeking new and revolutionary breakthroughs. This trend was personified in the Avro Lincoln, which, developed to specification B14/43 to meet a need for a Lancaster replacement, flew for the first time in June 1944 and entered service with

RAF Bomber Command in 1945, too late to see action in the war. The Lincoln, originally known as the Lancaster IV and V, was to remain the mainstay of Bomber Command until the early 1950s, when it began to be replaced by the English Electric Canberra. Some idea of the critical deficiency in Bomber Command's strategic delivery systems at this time may be gained from the fact that, beginning in 1950, 87 B-29s were loaned to the RAF to sustain its strategic capability until the V-Bombers entered service. In the United States, deliveries of the B-47 had already been made to Strategic Air Command.

The main reason why the British chose to develop existing designs, rather than divert valuable wartime resources to the development of new and advanced strategic bombers, was an understandable desire to make use of what was already in production to bring the war to an end as quickly as possible. The AOC-in-C Bomber Command, ACM Sir Arthur Harris, later admitted that he was influenced – and indeed frightened – by the possibility that the Germans were developing an atomic bomb, and that by maintaining a maximum effort offensive against the enemy's industry and communications he was buying time for the Allies. The sense of urgency left little time to worry about what equipment Bomber Command would have at its disposal in the postwar years.

Only when the war was over did the development of a new and effective strategic strike force for

Left: The Avro Lincoln saw service with the RAF well into the 1950s. It epitomised the British policy of developing existing designs to their limits rather than taking risks with new ventures. The Lincoln was not suitable for nuclear weapons' delivery and was considerably outdated when replaced by the V-force./*MoD*

Above: Shorts put forward a design to meet specification B35/46 – the marrying of an SA4 Sperrin's body to an isoclinic wing, which they designated the PD1. Not accepted, the Sperrin prototypes were used in the development of nuclear stores for the Valiant. Here the Sperrin is seen in its bombing configuration at the 1951 SBAC display./*MoD*

Bomber Command assume paramount importance, and it was clear that such a force must be capable of delivering nuclear weapons. It was also clear that such weapons would have to be of British design, for in August 1946 the McMahon Act, which forbade the disclosure of US nuclear information to other states, brought an effective end to Anglo-American nuclear collaboration. Britain did, however, retain access to some uranium sources, including those of the Congo, and in 1945-6, under the auspices of Clement Attlee's new Labour government, work was begun on a research and experimental establishment at Harwell, production reactors at Windscale and a low-separation diffusion plant at Capenhurst.

The decision to go ahead with the design of indigenous nuclear weapons was influenced by the belief of both Attlee and his senior ministers that the possession of such weapons would re-consolidate Britain's status as a world power. Although the East-West power blocs were already taking shape in 1946, there was no thought at this stage, in British minds at least, of using the bomb as a deterrent, or even that it might be effective as such.

It was not until the beginning of 1947 that the decision to produce atomic bombs was made by the British Government. In the meantime, however, the Air Staff, under the leadership of Lord Tedder, had drafted a requirement for a British nuclear bomb and the specification of an aircraft that would be capable of delivering it. Tedder was a strong advocate of economy of force; he argued that a British defence policy in peacetime should be directed towards the creation of a 'fully-grown David' rather than an 'embryo Goliath'. There could no longer be any question, in the nuclear age, of Britain becoming involved in a war of attrition; any future conflict must be fought by highly trained, highly mobile forces possessing great firepower. As far as Bomber Command was concerned, this meant the creation not of a bludgeon, but a rapier.

The first British strategic jet bomber specification was B35/46, conceived as an operational requirement in 1946 and issued at the beginning of 1947. This called for an aircraft capable of carrying a 10,000lb store at 500kts over a still-air range of 3,350nm, with a ceiling of 50,000ft over the target; its bomb load was to be doubled over shorter ranges and was to consist either of conventional weapons or a 'special' (ie nuclear) bomb accommodated internally. This meant that the bomb bay would have to house a weapon measuring 25ft in length by 5ft in diameter. The aircraft was to have a five-man crew, accommodated together in a jettisonable pressure cabin; pressure was to be maintained at 9lb/sq in, equivalent to an altitude of 8,000ft, during cruise to the target at 45,000ft, reducing to 3.5lb/sq in over the target to minimise the risk of explosive decompression if the aircraft sustained damage. The bomber was to be equipped with an advanced version of H2S for navigation and bombing, but a visual bombing station was also to be provided. Another requirement was that the aircraft was to be capable of being produced in quantity. Avro, Armstrong-Whitworth, Handley Page, Short Brothers and Vickers all submitted designs to meet the specification; Avro's and Handley Page's were the ones eventually selected by the Ministry of Supply.

A second specification, B14/46, was issued in August 1947, and was much less demanding than B35/46. It called for an aircraft with the same range, but with a lower ceiling (45,000ft) and speed (390kts compared to 500kts). Using a conventional straight wing design, this was intended as an insurance against delays in fulfilling the more advanced B35/46 specification. It was eventually to materialise in the Short SA4 Sperrin, of which more later.

For Britain's aircraft designers the strategic jet bomber requirement posed a whole new range of problems, not the least of which was that, in order to meet the specification fully, aerodynamic design knowledge would have to be pushed to its absolute limits, and perhaps even beyond. Research facilities, too, were greatly inferior to those existing in the United States; throughout the whole industry there was not a single transonic wind-tunnel, because although working examples had been discovered in Germany at the end of the war these had been dismantled with astonishing speed and shipped back to the USA, along with a vast amount of data on high-speed aerodynamics and design.

Nevertheless, the slender amount of German material that remained was to assist the British designers in performing near miracles. Armstrong-Whitworth, Avro, Bristol, English Electric, Handley Page, Short and Vickers all entered the running to meet B35/46, and each design with the exception of

Shorts' was influenced by German data. Shorts' submission, the PD1, was initiated by the firm's project designer David Keith-Lucas in 1947 and was basically an SA4 Sperrin front fuselage married to an aeroisoclinic wing, the tailplane being eliminated. At their own expense Shorts built a one-third scale glider, the SB1, which flew in 1951 and was later modified and fitted with two Turbomeca Palas turbojets. In this guise, as the SB4 Sherpa, it carried out extensive trials during the early 1950s, but the PD1 proposal was not accepted. Neither was Bristol's submission, the Type 172, which featured a wing swept at an angle of 45 degrees; preliminary design work began in October 1946 and was eventually abandoned two years later.

A. V. Roe and Company at Chadderton, Manchester, began serious design studies towards fulfilling the requirements of B35/36 in January 1947. For Roy Chadwick, Avro's technical director, and his design team the lack of information on high-speed flight and configurations, together with the absence of transonic research facilities, meant starting from scratch. First of all, they investigated a series of swept-wing designs, culminating in one with 45 degrees of sweep and swept tail surfaces, but discovered that such an aircraft would be well in excess of the 100,000lb weight limit imposed by B35/36 and would have a lower performance than that required. They therefore investigated ways to save weight and improve performance, and it seemed that an all-wing design might provide a favourable solution.

The idea was far from new. The Messerschmitt Me 163 rocket-propelled fighter had been an all-wing design, with no horizontal tail surfaces, and a lot of research into triangular wing shapes had been carried out in Germany by Dr Alexander Lippisch. The German firm of Horten had also experimented with all-wing aircraft, and the prototype of a fighter, the Ho9, had been nearing completion at the war's end. In Britain, De Havilland had flown their little tailless DH108 in May 1946, while Armstrong Whitworth, after experimenting with all-wing gliders, were building a jet-powered model, the AW52. Chadwick and his team were especially interested in American efforts in the all-wing field, which had produced an experimental four-engined bomber, the Northrop XB-35; this had flown in June 1946 and a jet-powered variant was mooted. (This was later to emerge as the YB-49, both prototypes of which exploded in mid-air during the test programme.)

Avro's early ventures into all-wing design soon showed that they were running into a severe weight penalty. It was clear that the only way in which the weight could be brought within the specification limits was to reduce the aspect ratio substantially

Above: Armstrong Whitworth's all-wing design, the AW52, was a jet-powered model of a previous glider. Roy Chadwick, Avro's technical director, used the AW52 flying controls on 'project No 698' – which was later to become the Vulcan. The AW52 in the photograph was the first of two prototypes built. It first flew from Boscombe Down on 13 November 1947, and crashed on 30 May 1949 with the pilot making the first ever British emergency ejection./*BAe*

Below: A.V. Roe's researches into providing the answer to specification B35/46 included the investigation of all-wing aircraft. The idea was far from new. De Havilland had built and flown such an aircraft – the DH108 which first flew on 15 May 1946. The first British aircraft to go supersonic, the DH108 never got further than the prototype stage./*MoD*

without a comparative reduction in wing loading; the result was a wing that was almost a pure triangle, like the Greek letter D – hence the universally adopted name 'Delta'.

The triangular wing that Chadwick's team now designed, under the project number 698, was a far cry from what it was later to become in the process of evolution. The crew compartment, housed under a blister canopy, was built into the apex of the triangle;

there was no projecting nose section. On either side of the wing's fat centre-section – deep enough for a man to stand upright inside it – two Bristol BE10 engines were to be buried, fed through two large circular air intakes projecting slightly ahead of the wing leading edge. Small, swept fins and rudders were mounted on the wingtips. The bombs were housed in bays situated between the engines and the main undercarriage, or, alternatively, they could be housed on one side only, with the space on the other side filled by extra fuel tanks. The flying controls were based on those fitted to the Armstrong-Whitworth AW52 and consisted of double elevons along the wing trailing edge.

The design was completed, apart from some minor modifications, by the end of March 1947, and in April it was decided to give the delta project full company backing. Detailed drawings were submitted to the Ministry of Supply the following month, and the Avro team settled down to await a decision.

Meanwhile, at Cricklewood in north London, the design team of Handley Page Ltd had been busily

Below: Carrying the US manned nuclear deterrent from the late 1950s, B-52 has proved longer lived than most jet bombers. Its life expectancy has been projected into the 1990s, and it has proved an adaptable and versatile design.

Above: Three generations of bomber – the Lancaster (this one ex-French Navy and returning to the UK for preservation), the Canberra (ex-RAAF) and the Victor (a K1A, XH591, of No 57 Squadron). Seen over Malaya in May 1965, the photograph gives a good indication of the relative sizes of the three aircraft./*John Hardy*

working up their own ideas on the B35/36 theme. Handley Page had long been interested in the tailless configuration, having built and flown an experimental aircraft, the Manx, in 1943, and when the chief designer, Reginald S. Stafford, went to investigate the achievements of Germany's wartime aircraft industry in June 1945, tailless research data was near the top of his shopping list. Four months later his deputy, Godfrey Lee, also went on an official mission to Germany to study tailless research on behalf of the Royal Aircraft Establishment, but he also took the opportunity to gather much material on the behaviour of various types of swept wing at high Mach numbers, all of which was duly passed on to Handley Page. Most of the German material in fact came from the Arado company, which had some very advanced high speed designs on the drawing board at the war's end. Armed with this new information, the small Handley Page team set about designing a jet-propelled, tailless bomber whose wings had a bold sweep – for that day – of 45 degrees and were tipped by vertical fins and rudders. Flaps were incorporated in the design, so to trim out the pitching moment a tailplane was mounted on a small fin at the mid-point of the wing.

This design, which anticipated B35/46 by several months, was submitted to the Ministry of Aircraft Production in June 1946, and no decision had been made about its future when Handley Page, together with five other companies, were invited to submit a tender to the specification on 1 January 1947. Logically, the design team turned to the original tailless bomber design as a basis for further study, but it was soon apparent that a modified wing shape would be necessary if the demands of the specification were to be met. Since neither the delta nor a thin swept wing seemed to offer the ideal solution Handley Page decided to combine the two, designing a wing with three different degrees of sweep, curving in a crescent from root to tip. Once again, the idea was not original; the Arado company had designed just such a wing shape in 1944.

The inboard, thickest part of the Handley Page wing was sharply swept at 53 degrees, the thickness/ chord ratio of 16% providing ample space for fuel, engines and main undercarriage, while at the tip the sweep was only 22 degrees, with a thickness/chord ratio of 6%. This shape, without doubt the most aerodynamically advanced of any on British drawing boards in 1947, enjoyed a number of big advantages, not the least of which that it had aeroisoclinic properties, eliminating a tendency to twist during high-g manoeuvres. By the end of 1947 the Handley Page design had assumed a more conventional appearance than the earlier tailless bomber, with a long fuselage, a tall, swept fin and rudder and a crescent-shaped, high-mounted tailplane. The aircraft, which was to have a crew of five, was to be powered by four 7,000lb thrust Metrovick F9 or Rolls-Royce AJ65 engines; gross weight was to be 90,000lb and, according to Handley Page estimates, it would be capable of carrying a 10,000lb bomb load over a still-air range of 5,000 miles at 520mph at 50,000ft. The design was allocated the type number HP80.

The official enthusiasm displayed over the 'futuristic' designs of both the Avro 698 and the HP80 almost strangled at birth the submission of the other contender for a B35/46 contract, Vickers-Armstrongs (Aircraft) Ltd. The Vickers design team at Weybridge, under the direction of Rex Pierson, had begun jet bomber studies in 1944, at the same time going ahead with the development of a new piston-engined bomber, the Windsor. Early in 1945 everything looked promising for the Windsor; three prototypes had been built and flown, four more were in hand and 300 production aircraft were on order. Then came the war's end, cancellation, and a halt to piston-engined bomber development, so Vickers accelerated their jet bomber programme under the direction of George R. Edwards, their new chief designer. Their proposal, the Vickers Type 660, was far more conventional in design than either the Avro or Handley Page aircraft, and although it offered vast performance and load-carrying increases over the Lincoln and the B-29 it nevertheless fell short of the B35/46 requirement, so in July 1947 it was rejected in favour of the rival designs.

The rejection was to be only temporary. Thanks in no small measure to the efforts of George Edwards, who eventually persuaded the authorities that the potential performance of the 660 was greatly outweighed by its ability to be developed more quickly, interest was once more awakened in the design and it was now regarded as an 'interim' aircraft, a kind of insurance against the failure of the more radical bombers.

It was a fortunate decision, and one which had far-reaching consequences. In March 1948, when a new specification (B9/48) was written around the Vickers 660, not even George Edwards could have dreamed of the role this aircraft would play over the years to come. This was the aircraft that would be the mainstay of the RAF's nuclear strike force during the dangerous years of the 1950s, and would pioneer the operational techniques of what was to become known as the V-Force. In service, it would chalk up an impressive eries of 'firsts'; it would become the only V-Bomber to drop bombs in anger; and it would be the only British aircraft to release nuclear weapons.

The name chosen for it was Valiant.

V-Bomber Genealogy

17 December 1946 Operational Requirement (OR229) for medium-range bomber finalised.
7 January 1947 OR229 issued.
Ministry of Supply Specification B35/46 issued.
9 January 1947 Avro, Armstrong-Whitworth, Bristol, English Electric, Handley Page and Short Brothers invited to tender.
28 July 1947 Tender design conference.
11 August 1947 MoS Specification B14/46 issued.
19 November 1947 Handley Page awarded HP80 prototype contract.
17 December 1947 Shorts given ITP (intention to proceed) on B14/46.
1 January 1948 Avro awarded Type 698 prototype contract.
16 April 1948 Vickers given ITP to build two prototypes.
19 July 1948 MoS Specification B9/48 issued.

The Valiant

Development and Testing

The new specification written round the Vickers Type 660, delineating its interim status, was B9/48, and in February 1949 two prototypes of the aircraft were ordered, one to be powered by Rolls-Royce Avon engines and the other by Sapphires, although it was later decided that both 660s should be fitted with Avons. Work on the aircraft had in fact already been started in April 1948, when the Ministry of Supply had issued an Instruction to Proceed (ITP), and now it continued round the clock, under conditions of the strictest secrecy, at Weybridge and Foxwarren, the Vickers dispersal plant where major components of most of the company's prototypes were built. In carrying out their task Vickers were fortunate in having some of the British aircraft industry's best research facilities, including a Mach 0.94 wind tunnel, installed in 1949.

The aircraft that gradually took shape was highly streamlined and, for its size, remarkably elegant. The 108ft fuselage was of circular section, with a large navigation and bombing radar installation (the largest, in fact, developed up to that time for a British aircraft) occupying the whole of the nose forward of the cockpit. A blister under the nose accommodated the visual bomb-aiming station. The pressurised crew compartment itself was built by Saunders-Roe, one of nine major sub-contractors involved in the Type 660 programme, and accommodated five crew members: pilot and co-pilot, two navigators and an air electronics officer. The last three sat below and behind the pilots, facing aft, and had no ejection seats; in the event of an emergency they would have to unfasten their seat harnesses and various leads and open the main hatch, together with a metal windbreak that hinged out of the fuselage side ahead of the door. Without the windbreak, an exit from the hatch at high speed would have been virtually impossible. The two pilots would make their exit by first jettisoning the cockpit roof, which was blown off by a series of explosive bolts, and then using their Martin-Baker Mk 3A seats.

In all fairness, it should be mentioned at this point that in its original Operational Requirement, the Air Staff asked that the complete pressure cabin accommodating the crew should be jettisonable in an emergency and equipped with parachutes to form an escape capsule, but the contracting companies found the engineering problems associated with providing such a system to be insuperable. In 1948 Handley Page actually tested such an escape system in model form, but the results were unsatisfactory and the idea was abandoned. Much later, in 1960, Martin Baker experimentally installed a rearwards-facing ejection seat in Valiant WP199, a CA (Controller of Aircraft) machine which had been modified for the purpose by Marshalls of Cambridge in 1959. There were delays in the programme because of pressure on Martin Baker for fighter aircraft ejection systems (they were developing one for the Lightning at that time) but trials eventually took place in mid-1960 and on 3 June that year a slave seat was successfully fired from the static aircraft at Chalgrove airfield. There was, however, no further development of the project, despite this initial success.

The Vickers Type 660's high-mounted wing had a mean sweep of 20 degrees, the angle being increased towards the wing root – at the thickest part – to improve lift-drag ratio. In this section the engines were buried. The structure of the wing, and indeed of the whole aircraft, was entirely conventional. In fact, the only major innovation lay in the electrical systems, with which the bomber was crammed. The main 112V DC system was supplied by four 22.5kW generators, one driven by each engine. Full voltage was obtained at all engine speeds from idling to take-off RPM. The generators charged a 96V battery and supplied power to the fuel pumps, undercarriage main and emergency motors, flap main and emergency motors, air brake motor, tailplane incidence motors, power controls hydraulic pump motors, brakes and nosewheel steering hydraulic pump motors, bomb door and airflow deflector motors, 28V rotary transformers, radar inverters and H2S scanners. Three 3kW rotary transformers were driven by the 112V supply; these charged the 24V battery and provided power for all services not powered by the high-voltage system. Most of the electrical equipment, and the main power

Top right: The first prototype of the Type 660, WB210, powered by four Rolls-Royce Avon RA3 turbojets made its first flight on 18 May 1951. Note the original slot intakes./*Rolls-Royce*

Right: First public appearance of WB210 – known as the Valiant from June 1951 – at the 1951 SBAC display. The aircraft crashed on 12 January 1952 following an engine fire./*MoD*

distribution panels, were housed in an upper compartment (known to crews as the organ loft) aft of the pressure cabin.

The prototype 660, WB210, was powered by four Rolls-Royce Avon RA3 turbojets of 6,500lb st. These were completely buried in the wing, with the tailpipes breaking the upper surface near the traiing edge. Originally, a single slot-type leading-edge intake in each wing fed air to each pair of engines, but some initial difficulties with engine running led to vertical straighteners being added to the intakes before the aircraft made its first flight.

Early in 1951, the components of the prototype Vickers 660 were taken from Foxwarren to the new company airfield at Wisley, in Surrey, where final assembly took place. After a period of systems testing and pre-flight trials, WB210 made its first flight on 18 May 1951, with Vickers' chief test pilot J. 'Mutt' Summers as captain and G. R. 'Jock' Bryce as co-pilot. Conditions were gusty and the flight lasted only five minutes. As a precautionary measure the undercarriage was locked down and the flaps were left at their take-off setting of 20 degrees throughout. Four more flights were made from Wisley, but as this was only a grass airfield the 660 was subsequently moved to Hurn while a runway was laid at the previous location.

In June 1951 the name Valiant was officially adopted for the Vickers design, and in 1952 it was decided that the Avro and Handley Page aircraft should have names beginning with 'V' as well. The establishment of a 'V' class of medium bombers was proposed by the then Chief of the Air Staff, Marshal of the Royal Air Force Sir John Slessor, and in October 1952 the Air Council decided on the name Vulcan for Avro's B35/46, followed by Victor for the Handley Page design in December. This was a break with long tradition; hitherto, RAF bomber aircraft had been named after inland towns in the British Commonwealth (eg Canberra) or towns associated with British history (eg Lancaster).

The Valiant flight test programme continued steadily with WB210 through the remainder of 1951. By this time a Royal Air Force officer, Sqn Ldr Brian Foster, had been attached to the Valiant test team, and on 12 January 1952 he was flying as co-pilot in the prototype, carrying out engine shutdown and relight trials over the Hampshire coast, when fire broke out in an engine bay as a result of a wet start. No fire detection equipment had been installed in the bay, and by the time the blaze was detected the damage was so advanced that the wing was on the point of collapse. The pilot therefore gave the order to abandon the aircraft and the three rear crew members went out first, followed by the two pilots. All the crew survived with the exception of Sqn Ldr Foster, who

died when his seat struck the fin while the aircraft was in a decending turn.

Fortunately for Vickers, the second prototype Valiant, WB215, was approaching completion at Foxwarren, and this flew for the first time at Wisley on 11 April 1952. Allocated Type Number 667, WB215 differed from its predecessor in having enlarged air intakes to feed the 7,500lb st Avon RA7 engines with which it was fitted. This aircraft sustained the test programme for more than a year and the Vickers team was joined by another RAF officer, Sqn Ldr Rupert G. W. Oakley.

Meanwhile, on 8 February 1951, Vickers had received an ITP for 25 production Valiant B Mk 1s, confirmed by a contract placed on 12 April. Five of these aircraft were to be powered by 9,000lb st Avon RA14 engines, while the remaining 20 were to have 10,500lb st Avon RA28s, with longer jet pipes. About the same time, the company had also received a Ministry of Supply specification for the development of a prototype target-marking version of the Valiant, which was to be specially strengthened in order to fly low and fast and was to have increased fuel tankage. Bearing the type number 673, the designation Valiant B Mk 2 and known unofficially as the Pathfinder, this aircraft flew for the first time on 4 September 1953, just in time for that year's SBAC show at Farnborough, where it was displayed in a resplendent glossy black overall finish. The B Mk 2's fuselage was 4ft 6in longer than that of the B1 and, because of major structural redesign to the wings, a bogie-type main undercarriage was housed in two long nacelles projecting behind the trailing edge.

The strengthened airframe, coupled with Rolls-Royce Avon RA14 engines, gave the B Mk 2 version an enormous performance advantage over the earlier Valiant. It could, for example, attain a maximum speed at sea level of 552mph, whereas the B Mk 1 version was limited by airframe considerations to 414mph. Performance of the production version, had it gone ahead, would have been even more impressive, for this was to have been powered by the Rolls-Royce RB80 by-pass engine, progenitor of the Conway turbofan. In the mid-1950s, however, the Air Staff decided that there was no longer a requirement for the role the Valiant B Mk 2 was to have fulfilled, and the sole example, WJ954, was eventually scrapped. Ironically, 10 years later the whole of the V-Force was compelled to adapt to the low-level role, and the airframes of the Valiants then in service were found to be incapable of withstanding the stresses imposed by prolonged flight at low level.

In the autumn of 1953, with the test programme now well advanced and the first production Valiant about to be rolled out, plans were made to enter the second prototype, WB215, in the London-

Right: WJ954 at the 1954 SBAC display. Note the undercarriage nacelles projecting behind the trailing edge – the main gear retracted upwards./*MoD*

Below: The second Valiant prototype, WB215, showing its paces at the 1952 SBAC display. Note the high surface finish and the revised 'spectacle' shaped intakes. WB215 was powered by RA7 engines and was broken up in March 1952./*MoD*

Bottom: WJ954, the first (and only) Valiant B2, is seen here landing at the 1953 SBAC display resplendent in glossy all-black 'night-interdictor' finish. With a longer fuselage than the B1, the B2 also boasted new four-wheel bogie undercarriage units permitting increased weight./*MoD*

Christchurch (New Zealand) air race in October that year. Some modifications were necessary, including the fitting of underwing fuel tanks with a capacity of 1,645 Imperial gal each, the installation of uprated Avons and certain changes to the navigational equipment. Incorporating these changes, WB215 received the new type number Vickers 709, but at the very last moment – mainly because no Valiant had yet made an overseas flight and therefore no information was available on the type's behaviour in tropical conditions – the Air Ministry decided to withdraw it from the running and it was left to English Electric's twin-jet Canberra light bomber to win the race. The modification programme, however, was not entirely wasted, for some of the innovations – particularly the underwing fuel tanks – were subsequently incorporated in production aircraft.

The first of the production Valiants, WP199, flew for the first time on 21 December 1953, well within the deadline imposed by the Ministry. At the controls were Jock Bryce and Brian Trubshaw, who many years later was to be the first Englishman to fly Concorde. The first five production Valiants (RA14-powered) were allocated the type number Vickers 674, and carried full radar. One of these aircraft was involved in a serious incident when both ailerons broke away during high-speed trials at medium level, but test pilot Bill Aston brought it safely back to Boscombe Down with a display of skill and airmanship that has seldom been equalled.

While the early production aircraft were being put through their paces at the various development establishments, production of the definitive Valiant B Mk 1 was getting under way. The first RA28-powered B1 (type number 706) was WP204, and this machine went to the Handling Squadron at Boscombe Down for acceptance trials on 4 April 1955. In 1954 came the first change in specification, with an order for 11 Valiants fitted with removable equipment for long-range, high-altitude photographic reconnaissance sorties by day or night and for aerial survey work. These were slotted into the production line at intervals, the first of them – designated Vickers Type 710 and Valiant B(PR)1 in RAF service – flying for the first time on 8 October 1954, bearing the serial WP205.

Later, when production of the B1 terminated with the 29th aircraft, yet another variant, the B(PR)K1, appeared on the production line, beginning with WZ376. This version was fitted with a flight refuelling hose-reel pack in the bomb bay and also with cameras; 14 were built, under the Vickers type number 733. Later still, all production switched to the BK1, in which the cameras were deleted. In addition to the bomb bay refuelling pack, this variant was fitted with a nose probe. The Vickers type number was 758, and 45 were issued to the RAF, beginning with WP214. (After brief service with No 138

Below left and above: Short SA4 Sperrin VX158 flying past
Farnborough's control tower during the 1956 SBAC display. After
losing its chances of production, the two Sperrin prototypes were
used for a variety of tests and trials at RAE./*MoD*

Squadron, WP214 subsequently became quite
famous in Bomber Command as the 'special' Valiant,
carrying large amounts of ECM and other electronic
equipment in the bomb bay. It shared its existence
between the Bomber Command Development Unit
and Vickers, where the necessary modifications were
carried out.)

In 1954, the disused airfield of Gaydon, in
Warwickshire, which had been used for bomber
aircrew training during the war, was reactivated and
extensively rebuilt to become the first V-Bomber
base. In January 1955 the Valiant received its CA
Release – ie clearance by the Controller (Aircraft) for
operational service in the UK and overseas – and in
June that year RAF Gaydon was designated No 232
Operational Conversion Unit, with the tasks of
carrying out Valiant intensive flying trials and training
crews for the V-Force. Many of the OCU's officers,
including Rupert Oakley – now a wing commander –
had been involved in the Valiant development
programme at Weybridge, Wisley and Boscombe
Down.

Following a similar policy to that of America's
Strategic Air Command, all crews selected for service
with the V-Force were to be veterans. Aircraft
captains had to possess an 'above average' rating and
had to have a minimum of 1,750 hours as first pilot;
second pilots (called co-pilots from 1958) were
required to have completed at least 700 hours as
captain, and both must have completed a tour on
Canberras. Navigators, too, had to have a Canberra
tour behind them, as well as a course at the Bomber

Command training school at Lindholme in
Yorkshire. Signallers – subsequently to be called Air
Electronics Officers, which more adequately
described their role – were required to have flown a
tour with Bomber, Transport or Coastal Command.
Originally, a V-Force tour lasted five years,
compared with 2½-3 years elsewhere, and crews
would often remain with the same squadron
throughout that period. Later, with an increase in the
demand for aircrew, the requirements for V-Force
service were to become less stringent. The V-Force
also introduced the American idea of the crew chief
to the RAF. Usually a Chief Technician, he would be
in charge of the ground crew assigned to an individual
aircraft throughout its career, and flew in the aircraft
on overseas trips.

Meanwhile, as No 232 OCU's first course worked
steadily towards qualification and the formation of an
operational Valiant squadron, an airfield had been
designated to receive the latter. This was RAF
Wittering, near Stamford, which had previously been
occupied by four Canberra light bomber squadrons.

It was at Wittering, in November 1953, that the
RAF had begun to stockpile its first operational
nuclear bombs. Ever since the British nuclear
weapons programme had been initiated in 1947,
development of an operational device had proceeded
independently of the aircraft that were to carry it, and
it had reached fruition a good deal sooner. The
overall direction of the nuclear weapons programme
had been in the hands of Lord Portal, the Controller
of Production of Atomic Energy, who had been the
RAF Chief of Air Staff throughout most of the war;
and the leader of the 10-man RAF team charged with
developing the weapon was Wg Cdr J. S. (later Air
Marshal Sir John) Rowlands. The RAF team worked
under Dr William Penney, Chief Superintendent of

Armament Research in the Ministry of Supply, and they had to start virtually from scratch, because only Dr Penney had had any kind of practical experience in the field, having worked on Project Manhatten in the United States during the war. They eventually assembled a device – not yet a bomb – and this was successfully tested at the Monte Bello Islands in the Pacific on 3 October 1952.

The design of an aerodynamically-suitable casing and an operational warhead went ahead during the winter of 1952-3, and dropping trials were carried out with bomb shapes constructed to various aerodynamic specifications. Since no Valiant was yet available, these early trials were caried out by the very aircraft whose hopes of production the Valiant had destroyed: the Short SA4 Sperrin.

Two Sperrin prototypes had been built and flown, the first on 10 August 1951. This aircraft, XV158, carried out numerous trials at the Royal Aircraft Establishment, Farnborough, some involving escape techniques which were subsequently applied to aircraft of the V-Force. It had, incidentally, been the original intention to fit the Sperrin with a jettisonable nose section to form a safety capsule for high-altitude escape, as specified in OR229, but trials with models had shown that severe tumbling would occur before the parachutes that supported the capsule deployed at 12,000ft, so the idea was dropped.

In the spring of 1953 VX158 carried out numerous operational trials of the new high-altitude radar navigational and bombing equipment that would eventually be incorporated in the Vulcan and Victor, markers being released through a small inset door in the bomb bay and a visual bombing station replacing the metal nose cone. On 11 April its sister aircraft, VX161, flew to RAF Woodbridge to begin trials with bomb shapes in connexion with the nuclear weapons programme, releasing payloads of up to 10,000lb at speeds of up to 0.78M and altitudes of up to 40,000ft. After carrying out further trials on behalf of the RAE both Sperrins were eventually scrapped, but not before they had made a significant – and nowadays forgotten – contribution to the development of V-Force equipment.

The assembly of Britain's first operational nuclear weapon, codenamed 'Blue Danube', continued throughout the summer of 1953. Even today, precise details of it can not be released; but it was a plutonium bomb, it weighed 10,000lb and it was 24ft in length, with a kiloton-range warhead. The latter was tested in its operational configuration at Woomera, Australia, on 14 October 1953, but it was to be another three years before an airdrop was carried out. In the meantime, a Valiant took over from the Sperrins in carrying out air tests of bomb shapes.

The first nuclear weapons delivered to Wittering

Above: This was the posture that had to be adopted by rear crew members during emergency exits from a Valiant. The eyelid-type windshield is clearly visible./*RAF*

Below: Valiant B1 XD823 prior to delivery to the RAF./*BAe*

Right: Valiant B(K)1 XD816 at Wisley during May 1967 – positively the last Valiant flying, this aircraft was undergoing a Ministry of Technology test programme when the other Valiants were grounded. *Centre:* A clear view of the take-off flap setting and (*top*) the tail markings which indicate that XD816 saw service with No 214 Squadron are well illustrated./*BAe*

became part of an intensive ground training programme that lasted throughout 1954. By the autumn of that year the station possessed a cadre of highly-trained technical personnel, skilled in the handling of what – for the RAF – was an entirely new type of armament, though the operational status of the weapon had yet to be confirmed by a live drop.

Meanwhile, the Wittering personnel eagerly awaited the introduction of the Valiant into full service. The first steps were taken when, in January 1955, Wg Cdr Oakley and the newly-qualified OCU course formed the nucleus of the first Valiant squadron, No 138. It received its first aircraft, Valiant B1 WP206 – taken over from the OCU – in February, and after a five-month working up period at Gaydon the squadron moved to Wittering with six aircraft in July.

At long last, the V-Force had teeth.

In Service

In operational service, the Valiant quickly endeared itself to its crews. The aircraft had no vices and handled pleasantly throughout the flight envelope. There were no complicated procedures. Engines were started in the order 3-2-1-4 (at a later date, a

Right: Crews of No 207 Squadron (Valiants) debrief at Malta following the night attacks on Egyptian targets during the Suez operations in November 1956./*RAF*

Top: Valiants WZ390 (a B(K)1) and WZ376 (a B(PR)K1) during early flight refuelling experiments from Boscombe Down in 1955. /*BAe*

Two views of Valiant XD818, the aircraft which dropped the first British H-bomb; (*top right*) at the 1959 Battle of Britain display RAF St Athan and (*far right*) now in camouflage on permanent display at RAF Marham./*John Hardy; RAF*

technique was evolved for starting all four at the same time) and the procedure was as follows:

Instrument master switch – ON
Throttle/HP cocks – Fully closed
LP master cocks – ON
   Fuel pumps – Two ON each side
        Fuel pressure warning lights OUT
Engine starter selector switch – To engine to be started
Engine starter master switch – START
No 2 radar inverter – ON

The starter button was then pressed and the throttle/HP cock lever moved to the idling position, the engine normally lighting up within 4-8sec. The aircraft was usually taxied with all four engines running and the flying controls locked, the crew using the handbrake in conjunction with the nosewheel steering rather than the toe brakes, which were quite sensitive. The minimum turning circle was about 100ft and pilots had to take care not to 'cut corners' while taxying, for severe damage could be caused to

the landing gear if the aircraft was allowed to pivot round one of the tandem main wheel units.

For take-off, the second pilot operated the engine, undercarriage and flap controls and also checked for engine malfunction. After completion of the pre-take-off checks, the aircraft was lined up on the runway and the throttles opened to 7,000rev/min for not longer than five seconds with the hand brake held fully on while the crew checked pressures and temperatures. The brakes were then released and the throttles opened fully, directional control being maintained by use of the nosewheel steering until rudder control became effective at about 70kts. At about 25kts before the unstick speed (which varied from 103kts at a take-off weight of 90,000lb to 144kts at 175,000lb) the control column was moved back smoothly to lift the nosewheel.

The normal procedure after take-off was to climb at 250kts until this speed coincided with 0.73M, the climb then being continued at 0.75M, which was also the recommended cruising speed. High speed flying produced no change in the Valiant's behaviour, apart from a nose-up change of trim which became marked at about 0.84M. Slight compressibility buffeting occurred at 0.8M. Application of g when turning at Mach numbers above 0.78 was not recommended, as it tended to produce severe buffeting which could have resulted in structural damage.

A normal descent, with throttles closed and airbrakes extended, was made at 240kts, giving a rate of descent of 3,500-4,000ft/min. The aerodrome circuit was usually joined at 190kts, the flaps lowered to 20 degrees and speed then maintained at 170kts until the aircraft was on the downwind leg. The speed was then further reduced to the appropriate value, depending on the aircraft's weight – 150kts at 110,000lb, for example. This speed was maintained until the aircraft was opposite the downwind end of the runway on a visual circuit (or until half a mile before the glide path was intercepted in the case of an instrument approach) and then the flaps were lowered to 40 degrees. The speed was once again reduced to the appropriate level on final approach (133kts at 110,000lb) and maintained until full flap

was selected between 200 and 300ft above the ground, when the speed was adjusted to the correct value for crossing the threshold (105kts for weights of up to 80,000lb, plus 5kts for every 10,000lb in excess.) The landing was normal, the engines being throttled back at about 50ft above the runway and touchdown made on the main wheels.

Once initial deliveries had been made to No 138 Squadron, re-equipment of other squadrons with the Valiant proceeded fairly quickly. The second unit to get the type was No 543 Squadron at Wyton, which had received its first aircraft at Gaydon after forming there on 1 June 1955. These were Mk 1 B(PR)s, developed for the photographic reconnaissance role, and they transformed the RAF's strategic reconnaissance capabilities almost overnight. In the day role, these aircraft carried up to eight main fan cameras and a tri-installation of three cameras to provide wide-angle cover, all with the exception of two of the wide-angle cameras mounted in a camera crate in the bomb bay. Behind this, in a fairing, was a survey camera, with the two oblique cameras of the wide-angle installation mounted above it. In the night role, the B(PR)1 carried five or six cameras in the camera crate, together with five or six photo-cell units. Photo-flashes were housed in a flash crate at the rear of the bomb bay.

While Nos 138 and 543 Squadrons worked up to full operational standard in their respective roles, No 232 Operational Conversion Unit continued to expand in 1955 and turn out more crews for the formation of new squadrons in 1956. Two more Valiant bases were set up during that year, at Marham and Honington, both within Bomber Command's No 3 Group, and five more Valiant squadrons were formed. The first of these was No 214, which, having previously been equipped with Lincolns, re-formed at Marham in March 1956 under the command of Wg Cdr L. H. Trent VC; it was joined, in May, by No 207 Squadron, which had formerly operated Boeing Washingtons. Each unit was established for eight aircraft.

Also in May 1956, another Valiant squadron formed alongside No 138 at Wittering; this was No 49, a former Lincoln unit which had been engaged in operations against Mau-Mau terrorists in Kenya before its disbandment in August 1955. In July, the formation of No 148 Squadron completed the establishment of the Marham Wing, while the first of the Honington Valiant squadrons, No 7, formed on 1 November, to be followed by No 90 in January 1957.

In 1956, a series of trials were carried out with the aim of improving the efficiency of the RAF's medium bomber force, as the V-Force was alternatively known (the 'medium' referring to range, rather than size and weight). To improve the Valiant's

performance out of short strips at maximum weight, particularly under tropical conditions, tests were carried out with Scarab rockets clipped to the rear fuselage; these were later replaced by de Havilland Super Sprites, powered by a highly volatile mixture of high-test peroxide and kerosene and delivering a thrust of 4,200lb for 40sec. Because of a variety of problems, including lengthy scorch marks down the fuselage sides, these were relocated under the main engines, packaged in nacelles which – in theory at least – were reusable. The pack incorporated a steel strap with a pull of 300lb, which was used to stabilise it after release; negative-incidence foreplanes then rotated it into a nose-down attitude and a parachute then deployed, the landing being cushioned by automatically-inflated air bags. The whole system was tested on a Bristol Brigand at Boscombe Down and there was a trial installation on the second prototype Valiant, WB215; this aircraft, so equipped, was demonstrated by Brian Trubshaw at the 1956 SBAC show. Further trials were carried out between 23 August and 7 October 1958 by the Bomber Command Development Unit at Wittering, using three Valiants: WZ402 and XD871/2, which made eight assisted take-offs in all. However, although some preparations had been made for the use of RATO by V-Force squadrons, the system was not put into service because of the greatly increased engine thrust which became available with the Bristol Olympus and Rolls-Royce Conway.

In June 1956, Valiants went overseas for the first time when two aircraft – one from No 214 Squadron and one from No 543 – flew to Idris, in Libya, to take part in Exercise 'Thunderhead', testing the air defences of NATO countries in southern Europe and the Mediterranean area. Detachments overseas subsequently became routine, and in carrying them out the Valiant squadrons logged an impressive number of 'firsts'. It was a Valiant of No 214 Squadron, for example, which carried out the first non-stop trans-Atlantic flight by a V-bomber, flying from Loring Air Force Base (Maine) to Marham in 6hr 15min on 1 September 1956.

It was a Valiant, too, which made the first air drop of a British nuclear weapon. In August 1956, two aircraft of No 49 Squadron were detached to RAAF Edinburgh Field, and on 11 October Valiant WZ366, captained by Sqn Ldr E. J. G. Flavell, released the 10,000lb weapon from 35,000ft at 0.8M over the test range at Maralinga, South Australia. Also involved in

Top right: Crews leaving their Valiants during a 'Kinsman' exercise. Note entry door under cockpit./*RAF*

Right: Valiant B(K)1s of No 148 Squadron with their air and groundcrews before a daily demonstration of QRA scrambles at the 1960 SBAC display./*MoD*

the nuclear weapons trials was a Canberra B6 detachment from No 76 Squadron, whose base in the UK was Weston Zoyland; their task was to take atomic cloud samples at all altitudes, and for this work the Canberras were fitted with special filter equipment.

Meanwhile, political events decreed that some Valiant crews would shortly be called upon to put their operational efficiency to the test in earnest, albeit in a conventional bombing role. During October 1956, Valiants of Nos 138, 148, 207 and 214 Squadrons were detached to Luqa, Malta, and on 31 October their crews were briefed to attack Egyptian airfields as part of the air offensive that was to precede the Anglo-French landings in the Suez Canal zone, designed to seize key objectives and to separate the belligerent Egyptian and Israeli forces. The first series of attacks was carried out by Canberras of Nos 12 and 109 Squadrons and Valiants of Nos 148 and 214 against airfields in the Nile Delta (Almaza, Cairo West and Inchas) and in the Canal Zone (Abu Sueir, Fayid, Kabrit and Kasfareet). As they headed for their objectives, the RAF crews knew that the Egyptian air defences would be on the alert, because for some hours both Cyprus and Cairo Radios had been warning the Egyptian population that a series of attacks on airfields near Cairo and in the Canal Zone would begin following the expiry of the Anglo-French

ceasefire ultimatum to Israelis and Egyptians, the latter having rejected it.

The anticipated reaction from the Egyptian defences, however, failed to materialise. Visual navigation presented no problem, for every town in the Nile Delta was ablaze with light, and the crew of Valiant XD815 of No 148 Squadron – flying a mission from Malta that involved a five-hour, 1,800-mile round trip with an average of 15 minutes spent over enemy territory – had no difficulty in picking out the airfield at Almaza, their objective. This airfield had already been bombed by a Canberra of No 10 Squadron operating from Cyprus and was clearly marked by clusters of red target indicators. Valiant XD815 – the first V-bomber to drop bombs in anger – released its load of 1,000lb at 19.02hrs. Some anti-aircraft fire was observed, but the bursts were a long way below the attacking aircraft.

Subsequent Valiant operations over Egypt followed the same pattern, the aircraft bombing singly from about 40,000ft. Some bomber captains made two runs over the target to ensure adequate identification, great emphasis having been placed on reducing Egyptian casualties to a minimum. All the targets were marked by red TIs, dropped by 'Pathfinder' Canberras. Throughout the entire series of air attacks only one crew reported sighting an enemy night fighter, believed to be a Meteor NF13; it

fired two inaccurate bursts of tracer at a Valiant of No 148 Squadron. The Valiant pilot, Sqn Ldr E. T. Ware, took rapid evasive action and lost his attacker.

Attacks on major Egyptian airfields continued in strength for two more nights, and during the hours of daylight the pressure was maintained by Fleet Air Arm and French Navy fighter-bombers. Towards the end, the night bombing missions were carried out from medium level, which permitted much greater bombing precision, and were generally attended by more success than had been the case when the raids started. In an endeavour to keep casualties to a minimum, personnel at all Egyptian airfields were warned well in advance by Cyprus Radio that raids were imminent.

Operations by RAF Valiants and Canberras during the night of 1/2 November involved attacks on Cairo West airfield, which was bombed for the first time by the Valiants of No 138 Squadron, led by Wg Cdr Rupert Oakley DSO, AFC, DFM. There was no enemy opposition and the bombing was highly accurate, several sticks falling across the runway intersections. In all cases, pre-strike and post-strike reconnaissance was carried out by the Canberra PR7s of No 13 Squadron, which brought back so much information that the RAF Intelligence specialists were hard pressed to process it all in time. Moreover, tactical air reconnaissance, which had functioned like a well-oiled machine during the latter part of World War 2, had been allowed to gather cobwebs for some time, and the air operations had been in progress for a good 48 hours before an efficient processing system had been worked out.

Left: V-force on parade – Valiants, Victors and Vulcans./*RAF*

Top: Valiant WZ390 of No 214 Squadron, RAF Marham, with Bloodhound SAMs in the background./*RAF*

Below: Valiant B1 WZ363 landing at Wittering./*RAF*

The Valiant squadrons returned to the UK immediately after the Anglo-French landings in the Canal Zone, their task of helping to neutralise the Egyptian airfields completed. Setting aside all political considerations connected with the Suez operation, from the purely technical standpoint it had been a useful exercise for the RAF's new medium bomber force, confirming some old theories and initiating a few new ones. One of the things which did emerge, from that single brief encounter with an Egyptian Meteor, was that the Valiant possessed a sufficiently high ceiling and rate of climb to evade what was one of the standard night fighters of the period; another was that there was a tendency for part of the HE bomb load to 'hang up', but this had already been a source of frustration on many a practice bombing sortie. Bomb release, in fact, had been one of the very few snags encountered during trials with the Valiant; in the early days, it had been found that at high speed, the bombs tended to stay with the aircraft immediately after release, suspended a few feet under the bomb bay in the airflow, and considerable buffeting had also been experienced with the bomb doors open. To reduce buffeting, a deflector had been fitted at the rear of the bomb bay, and the bomb doors would not open until this was

raised. The bomb doors were controlled by a switch on the central pedestal between the two pilots; when this was set in the 'open' position the deflector rose and, as soon as it reached the fully up position, the bomb doors opened. Alternatively, the whole bombing sequence could be carried out automatically by the navigational bombing system, the controls of which were at the radar navigatator's position. When the appropriate switch was set to 'auto' the bomb bay deflector rose and, when it reached the fully up position, made a connection between the bomb door opening circuit and the navigational bombing control. In front of the bomb bay there was an air spoiler consisting of four vertical slats, which was extended prior to bomb release in order to break up the airflow under the bomb bay. This was particularly important when the 10,000lb MC Mk 1 nuclear store (Blue Danube) was carried, because the aerodynamic characteristics of this streamlined weapon required smooth release and separation from the aircraft.

The Suez crisis had led to the recall of the No 49 Squadron detachment from the nuclear weapons trials in Australia as a precautionary measure, and the beginning of 1957 found all the Valiant squadrons formed so far located at their UK bases. In July 1957, No 199 Squadron – which had been operating a mixture of Canberras and Lincolns in an ECM role – received its first Valiant at Honington. On 16 December 1958 it moved to RAF Finningley and its identity was changed to No 18 Squadron, where it operated six Valiants and a few Canberras. For a time, No 18 Squadron was responsible for electronic countermeasures for the whole of the V-Force. The squadron's Valiants carried one navigator and two AEOs, one of whom was responsible for operating the specialised ECM equipment.

Valiant production ended in 1957, the last aircraft – XD875 – being delivered on 24 September. By this time Vickers had built 108 production aircraft, plus two prototypes and the solitary Mk 2. Of this total, 14 were B(PR)K1s, the majority of which went to No 543 Squadron and which were equipped to receive fuel in flight, and 45 were BK1s, most of which were equipped to act both as tankers and receivers. The first flight refuelling trials with Valiants had taken place at Boscombe Down in November 1955, using two specially modified aircraft – WZ390 acting as tanker and WZ376 as receiver – but it was not until March 1958 that operational trials were initiated by

Left: B(K)1 of No 148 Squadron on the Farnborough runway during the 1960 QRA demonstration./*Peter Gilchrist*

Below: B1 WZ376 used by Vickers for flight refuelling experiments seen at Wisley. Note cutaway bomb bay and drogue just visible above port rear landing wheel./*Peter Gilchrist*

No 214 Squadron. This Marham-based unit subsequently became the RAF's first tanker squadron, pioneering a whole range of single-point flight refuelling techniques, using the probe-and-drogue system developed by Flight Refuelling Ltd.

In 1957, the most significant event in the development of the V-Force's deterrent potential was without doubt the testing of the first British thermonuclear device. In February 1955, the Statement on Defence had announced that the British Government had decided to proceed with the development and production of thermonuclear weapons, following the American H-bomb tests of 1954 and with the knowledge that the Soviet Union was pursuing a similar policy. Also in 1955, discussions had been opened with the Americans on nuclear co-operation for defence purposes, covering training and joint operations. It was the first significant breakthrough in this respect since the McMahon Act of 1946 had ended Anglo-American nuclear collaboration, and seems to have been influenced by the fact that Britain had since then created an independent nuclear capability.

So, with the help of some information released by the Americans, the British thermonuclear weapons programme went ahead, and by May 1957 an experimental megaton-range assembly was ready for testing. Once again, No 49 Squadron was detailed to carry out the air-drop, and in March 1957 four

Left and above: B(K)1 WZ397 convertible bomber/PR aircraft capable of receiving but not delivering fuel, seen over Biggin Hill, September 1964; note No 543 Squadron marking on underwing tank./*Peter Gilchrist*

Bottom: Another view of XD818, a B(K)1 of No 49 Squadron, which dropped Britain's first H-bomb./*Peter Gilchrist*

Valiants were detached to Christmas Island in the south-west Pacific. Many preparations had to be carried out before the actual drop was undertaken, such as the installation and checking of telemetry equipment, and the Valiant crews underwent two months of intensive training. There could be no room for errors; weapon release was to be from 39,000ft at a speed of 0.82M, followed by a steep turn through 90 degrees to get clear of the target area, which meant that the Valiant would have to be flown to its limits. The weapon was barometrically fused to detonate at 15,000ft over Malden Island, which was 350 miles south of Christmas Island.

That island – so named because Captain Cook landed there in HMS *Resolution* on Christmas Eve 1777 – may have sounded romantic to those who had never been there. In fact, it was a classic coral island, made habitable for the trials by the efforts of the Royal Engineers. Though humidity was high, trade winds made the climate bearable. Like other temporary residents, No 49 Squadron crews soon made the acquaintance of the indigenous gerboa rats and the numerous land and hermit crabs that thrive there. Nevertheless, morale throughout the entire Operation 'Grapple' task force was at its peak, with complete inter-Service integrity. To provide some relief from the somewhat primitive living conditions, the RAF contingent were entertained regularly on the task force command ship, the light aircraft carrier HMS *Warrior*.

On the morning of 15 May 1957, Valiant XD818, captained by Wg Cdr K. G. Hubbard, officer commanding No 49 Squadron, took off from Christmas Island with a prototype megaton-range weapon in its bomb bay. At 11.38, local time, the device detonated on schedule over Malden Island, producing a yield of approximately one megaton.

Above left: Valiant WZ392, a B(PR)K of No 543 Squadron, displaying its multiple camera and sensor windows during a low pass at Upavon during June 1962./*Peter Gilchrist*

Left: B(K) 1 XD825 of No 49 Squadron used on Operation 'Grapple', the Christmas Island H-bomb trials unit./*Peter Gilchrist*

Bottom left: Valiant B1 WP221 of No 207 Squadron at Biggin Hill during September 1963. Note lack of refuelling probe./*Peter Gilchrist*

Above: WZ395, a B(K)1 of No 148 Squadron, in low-level camouflage – the Valiants lost their white paintwork in 1963. This aircraft was originally allotted to No 214 Squadron and used by them during the Suez campaign of 1956./*Peter Gilchrist*

Within an hour of the air burst, Fleet Air Arm helicopters from HMS *Warrior* were lifting samples of radioactive soil from the island; these were flown to the carrier, on station 20 miles away. A TBM-3 Avenger, waiting on the carrier's catapult, took them to Christmas Island, where they were transferred to a Hastings transport aircraft. The latter ferried them to Honolulu, from where RAF Canberras flew them to the UK via the United States and Canada.

Three more tests with British thermonuclear weapons were carried out from Christmas Island in 1957, the last two air-drops being made on 19 June and 8 November. All involved warheads in the megaton range. (In fact, codenames for British thermonuclear devices were subsequently applied to the warheads rather than to the complete weapons.) Today, Valiant XD818, which began the series of tests, is preserved at RAF Marham, in Norfolk.

In October 1957, two Valiants – one from No 138 Squadron and the other from No 214, together with two Vulcans – represented RAF Bomber Command in the USAF Strategic Air Command Bombing Competition, held at Pinecastle Air Force Base in Florida. It was the first time that V-Force aircraft had

taken part in this competition, which lasted for six nights and involved 45 SAC bomber wings, each one represented by two aircraft and two crews, each of which flew on three alternate nights. The route, flown at level cruise, was more than 2,700 nautical miles long and included an astro navigation leg of over 800 miles and three widely spaced simulated bombing attacks. There were strict limitations, including a take-off 'window' of five minutes and an en route tolerance of plus or minus three minutes; failure to meet these automatically disqualified a crew, as did the failure to achieve a competition total of six scored bomb runs and two scored astro runs.

The two Valiants that took part were among the first to be delivered to the RAF complete with underwing fuel tanks, and were resplendent in their new white anti-flash finish. The competition began on 30 October and ended on 5 November, the RAF crews arriving three weeks early in order to familiarise themselves with SAC procedures and target data. The three targets were very precise. The first was the base of the north-east corner of the Columbian Steel Tank Company building in Kansas City; the second the centre of the turntable in the railway marshalling yards at St Louis; and the third the top of the north-west corner of the General Services warehouse in Atlanta. Despite some initial difficulty with the navigational bombing system in one of the Valiants, their final placing was 27th out of the total of 45 teams involved, one of the Valiant crews from No 214 Squadron (Sqn Ldr Ronald Payne) being placed 11th out of a total of 90 in the individual crew scoring part of the contest. Considering the quality and quantity of the opposition, it was a very satisfactory result.

Although 1957 and 1958 saw the introduction of the first Vulcan and Victor Squadrons, it was the Valiant

that continued to form the mainstay of the RAF's strategic deterrent to the end of the decade. At the beginning of 1961 the type still equipped nine squadrons and No 232 OCU; the Valiant squadrons still operational as part of the medium bomber force were Nos 7, 18 (still with its primary ECM role), 49, 90, 138, 148, 207 and 543 (strategic reconnaissance), while No 214 still had its tanker role; it was joined in this by No 90 Squadron, which became part of the tanker force at Marham from 1 October 1961.

During 1960-61 three Valiant squadrons, Nos 207, 49 and 148, were assigned to NATO in the tactical bombing role under the control of the Supreme Allied Commander, Europe (SACEUR). For this task the Valiants could be armed with either conventional bombs (a full load comprising 21 1,000lb in three clutches of five and two of three) or tactical nuclear weapons of American design.

In 1963, the Valiants lost their white paintwork and were camouflaged for the low-level role. Although

Left: Another B(K)1 of No 49 Squadron used on Operation 'Grapple'. XD825 is seen here at Wisley during the latter part of 1964. The decision to use Valiants in the low-level role led to stresses on the airframe, for which the aircraft had not been designed. During 1964 a fracture occurred in the rear spar of a Valiant and XD825 was used for engineering assessment of this spar fatigue./*BAe*

Below left: Another view of XD825 giving good detail of the flap area and the unusual undercarriage of the Valiant ./*BAe*

Below: Valiants awaiting their turn to be scrapped at Marham./*RAF*

the aircraft had never been designed to withstand the stresses imposed by this type of work, it was believed that its useful life would extend for a further five years. During 1964, however, a fracture occurred in the rear spar of a Valiant, and when other aircraft were inspected indications of metal fatigue were found. The last Valiant sorties were flown in December and the force was withdrawn from service in January 1965. At the end of 1964 there were six Valiant squadrons still in service: Nos 90 and 214 (tankers), Nos 49, 148 and 207 (SACEUR-assigned) and 543 (strategic reconnaissance). Of the others, No 7 had been disbanded in October 1962, No 138 in March 1962 and No 18 in March 1963.

Appropriately, one of the last Valiants to fly operationally was XD818 of Operation 'Grapple' fame. It took off from Marham on its last training sortie on 9 December 1964. The following month, work began on reducing all Valiants with the exception of 818 and four others – the latter engaged on special trials – to scrap. The last Valiant to fly was XD816, which had been on extended loan to the British Aircraft Corporation since September 1964 and which, on 29 April 1968, took part in a flypast to mark the disbandment of RAF Bomber Command and the inauguration of its successor, Strike Command. For the aircraft which had formed the core of Britain's nuclear deterrent for so long, it was a fitting swan song.

The Vulcan

Development and Testing

The summer of 1947, during which the Avro design team awaited a decision from the Ministry of Supply as to whether their Type 698 was to proceed, was marred by a tragedy that was deeply felt throughout the company. On 23 August, Roy Chadwick, Avro's Technical Director, was killed when G-AGSU, the prototype of the Tudor 2 airliner, crashed on take-off. This caused certain repercussions in the Ministry, where it was felt that the loss of all Chadwick's expertise might reflect unfavourably on the future development of the delta-wing bomber, but despite such fears, the company received an instruction to proceed with the building of two prototypes in January 1948, although a contract was not awarded until 28 July that year.

The design that now appeared on the drawing boards at Manchester was much altered from the original conception, for the Avro team had not ceased in their efforts to improve and refine the 698. In the closing weeks of 1947, wind tunnel tests at Farnborough showed the need for reducing the thickness/chord ratio of the 698's wing, which in turn led to other design changes. It had originally been planned to situate the bomber's Bristol BE10 engines in superimposed pairs, but a substantial reduction in the thickness of the wing made this idea impossible and the engines were re-located side by side. The plan to have two bomb bays in the wings was also dropped, that space being taken up by the repositioned engines, and a single weapons bay was built into a ventral bulge. A nose was also added, projecting some distance ahead of the wing and housing crew, radar and some of the fuel. Further design changes, in 1948, included the disappearance of the wingtip fins and their replacement by a central fin and rudder; the original elevons were also deleted and replaced by elevators and ailerons. The engine intakes were redesigned too, taking on a rectangular appearance.

Since little information was available on either the low- or high-speed handling characteristics of Avro's revolutionary design, the Ministry of Supply decided, during 1948, to order two one-third scale research aircraft to test the behaviour of the Type 698's configuration throughout the flight envelope. To investigate low-speed handling, Avro embarked on the design of the Type 707, powered by a single Rolls-Royce Derwent engine, while the Type 710, fitted with two Avons, was to carry out high-speed and high-altitude tests. The Type 710 was later abandoned, its place in the test programme being taken by a modified variant of the 707, the 707A.

Construction of the prototype Avro 707, to Specification E15/48, was started in the summer of 1948. The aircraft was astonishingly simple, using components from other aircraft wherever possible. The main undercarriage, for example, came from an Avro Athena trainer, while the cockpit canopy was 'borrowed' from a Meteor. There was no provision for an ejection seat. The 3,500lb st turbojet was mounted in the rear fuselage, with the fuel tank ahead of it, the engine intakes being situated on top of the fuselage on either side of the dorsal fairing.

The prototype Avro 707, VX784, was completed at Woodford in August 1949 and, following ground testing and taxying trials, was taken by road to Boscombe Down. The first flight, which lasted a little over half an hour, was made on the morning of 6 September, with Avro test pilot Flt Lt Eric Esler at the controls. Two more flights were made during the next two days, totalling two and a half hours, and Esler reported that the little aircraft behaved well. It was then flown to Farnborough to take part in the static display at the SBAC show, after which it returned to Boscombe Down for the installation of data measuring equipment. This was checked out during the 707's third flight in the last week in September, and all appeared set for the test programme to get under way when disaster struck. On 30 September, for reasons which were never clear, the aircraft crashed near Blackbushe and Esler was killed.

A study of the possible causes of the crash showed that there was no reason to doubt the basic soundness of the tailless delta concept, and work went ahead on the second Type 707, VX790. Unlike its ill-fated predecessor, this aircraft was fitted with an ejection seat and also incorporated other changes, including a

Top right: VX784, the first prototype Avro 707. This aircraft first flew on 4 September 1949 from Boscombe Down and it appeared at the 1949 SBAC display. Only 26 days after its first flight it crashed, killing the pilot, Eric Esler./*BAe*

Right: VX790, the second Type 707 designated 707B. Similar to VX784, it had a dorsal intake, was designed for low speed trials and first flew on 6 September 1950./*MoD*

Top left: WD280, the first Avro 707A. Its first flight was made on 14 June 1951 with Roly Falk in the cockpit. Designed for high speed trials with a new wing and intake, it is now preserved in Australia. */MoD*

Centre left: Avro 707C WZ744. The last of the 707 series to fly (first on 1 July 1953) and the only two-seater, the 707C was built for pilot familiarisation. It is now preserved at RAF Cosford./*BAe*

Bottom left: WZ736, the fourth of the series to fly (first on 20 February 1953), was the second 707A, similar in every respect to WD280. It is now preserved at RAF Cosford./*MoD*

Above: Flypast of four 707s and the two prototype Vulcans at the 1953 SBAC display./*BAe*

redesigned air brake system and modifications to the elevators. The installation of new equipment called for a new nose, and instead of designing one from scratch the Avro team decided to use that intended for the Avro 707A high-speed research aircraft. The nose was quickly built and fitted to VX790, which was then redesignated Avro 707B. Whereas the first 707 had used a nosewheel unit taken from a Meteor, the 707B was fitted with a nosewheel which had once belonged to a Hawker P1052 research aircraft.

The completed 707B was taken by road to Boscombe Down in August 1950, and it was hoped that the aircraft would fly in time to take part in that year's SBAC show. The machine was finally ready in the late evening of 5 September, and Wg Cdr R. J. 'Roly' Falk, who had recently joined the Avro team, decided to carry out some preliminary taxi trials, even though it was too dark to see clearly in the cockpit. The runway lights were switched on and Falk reached a high enough speed to lift the nosewheel and make a 'hop' of a few yards before shutting down for the night. The first real flight was made the following day, and lasted 15 minutes. Falk was so delighted with the handling of the little blue Type 707B that he immediately telephoned Sir Roy Dobson, Managing Director of A. V. Roe, and Air Marshal J. N. Boothman, the Controller of Supplies (Air) requesting permission to fly to Farnborough so that the aircraft could appear in the static display. Approval was readily granted and Falk arrived over Farnborough at the close of the first day's display, causing the homebound crowds to pause for a few minutes as he circled overhead, allowing the giant Bristol Brabazon to clear the runway, before making a straight, low approach and streaming the 707B's anti-spin parachute just after touchdown to reduce the landing run.

Systematic flight trials with the 707B were begun the week after the Farnborough show, the aircraft's behaviour being investigated over a speed range of 80-350kts at Boscombe Down and, later, at Dunsfold. To reduce the 707B's take-off run, which was unduly long because there was no angle of incidence between the fuselage and the ground and the elevators only began to 'bite' just short of unstick speed, the length of the nosewheel leg was increased by nine inches, which improved matters considerably. Inevitably, a lot of flying hours were spent investigating handling characteristics which had no direct relevance to the Avro 698 programme. For example, it was discovered that the 707B's dorsal intake suffered from air starvation at high speed,

caused by turbulence from the cockpit canopy, and modifications had to be made before the full range of flight trials could be undertaken satisfactorily; also, the aircraft's pitching oscillations called for a lot of investigation as a result of out-of-phase movement of the manual elevators, even though no similar problem would arise with the Type 698, which was to have powered flight controls.

Nevertheless, the 707B did contribute much useful information to the 698 programme, as a result of which some structural design changes were made, including the angling of the jet-pipe nozzles to compensate for longitudinal stability and trim variations with different power settings. The fin area was also decreased. The Type 707B was eventually

sent to Boscombe Down in September 1951 after completing about 100 hours research flying for Avro, and put in further useful work there during 1952.

Avro had received a firm contract for the building of two prototype 698s in July 1948, but detailed design work had been temporarily slowed down, for two reasons. The first was that the company was heavily involved in other projects, mainly the Shackleton maritime patrol aircraft, and drawing office space was limited; the second was that the high-speed Avro Type 707A had yet to fly, and the design team wanted to be in possession of its research data before taking any further big steps with the 698. In any case, as time went by it was becoming more and more probable that the engine proposed for the Type 698, the Bristol BE10 (now named Olympus) would not be ready in time, and consideration had to be given to possible alternatives, including Armstrong Siddeley Sapphires and Rolls-Royce Avons. Late in 1949, some redesign of the wing was also recommended as a result of wind tunnel tests at the Royal Aircraft Establishment, the engine air intakes now being blended into the wing root.

To test the new wing and intake design, a decision was taken in 1950 to go ahead with the building of the Avro 707A under Specification E 10/49. The configuration of this aircraft was much closer to that of the 698, with ailerons and elevators to scale and servo tabs and balances to assist the manual controls. With Roly Falk once again in the cockpit, the 707A – WD280 – flew for the first time from Boscombe Down on 14 July 1951, and by May the following year it had flown some 92 hours on research work. It went to Australia in 1956, where it was used for aerodynamic research. It was later preserved and put on display in Melbourne.

Two more aircraft in the Type 707 series were built by Avro. The first was another 707A, WZ736, which flew on 20 February 1953 and was used for automatic throttle development with the RAE; it was finally withdrawn in 1967 and went to the museum at RAF Finningley. The second was the 707C, which was originally designed as the prototype of a side-by-side, two-seat delta trainer. The sole aircraft, WZ744, flew

Top left: VX770, the first prototype Vulcan flying at the SBAC display of 1952. Then called the Avro 698, the classic delta wing with its straight leading edge was 'kinked' for the production Vulcans. This aircraft broke up in flight during a display at Hucknell in 1967. */MoD*

Above left: Vulcan B1 XA892, the fourth production aircraft, fitted with the initial version of the 'kinked' wing. This aircraft was allocated to armament trials and spent most of its life as a ministry research machine./*MoD*

Top: Avro 707A WD280 landing at Farnborough where it was used for some years as a general research aircraft./*MoD*

Right: Grp Capt Finch, former OC RAF Waddington, climbs from a Vulcan at RAAF Richmond after a trans-Australia flight. Note the proximity of the door to the nose oleo./*RAAF*

on 1 July 1953 and spent most of its working life in the development of power controls and electronics equipment at the RAE; it, too, was withdrawn in 1967 and ended its days in the RAF museum at Cosford. Neither of these aircraft made a contribution to the development of the Avro 698.

Meanwhile, the various components of the Avro 698 prototype, construction of which had got under way in 1951, had been transported to Woodford at the end of that year to await assembly. It was now certain that the Olympus engines would not be ready, because they were still undergoing ground-running tests, so the 6,500lb st Rolls-Royce Avon RA3 was selected instead. By August 1952, when Avro received a production contract, all the bits and pieces had been fitted together and the Avro team were working day and night to get the big delta ready for the SBAC display in September.

It was an impressively beautiful aircraft that finally emerged from the big assembly hangar at Woodford in the last week of August, resplendent in gleaming white paintwork and bearing the roundels of the Royal Air Force. It was to be given an official name four weeks later: Vulcan.

On 30 August Roly Falk climbed into the fighter-like cockpit of the prototype, VX770, and prepared to make the maiden flight. It was the biggest, most unconventional aircraft he had ever encountered, but his experience with the 707s had given him great

Above and below: During a goodwill visit by three Vulcan B1s of No 617 Squadron to New Zealand in October 1959, XH498 undershot while making a landing at Rongotai (Wellington airport). Sustaining damage to the port undercarriage, part of which pierced a port fuel tank, the aircraft successfully pulled up and flew back to Ohakea where it landed safely. Repaired in situ XH498 eventually returned to the UK seven months later./*RAF*

confidence and one fast taxi run was enough to satisfy him with regard to handling on the ground, wheel shimmy and nosewheel lifting speed. There was some delay in the take-off while a large flock of seagulls was dispersed from the runway area, but then Falk opened the throttles and the 698 began to roll, lifting into the air after a remarkably short take-off run. Falk, who was flying solo because a second pilot's seat had not yet been fitted, allowed himself plenty of height before raising the undercarriage, just in case there was any unexpected change of trim, and climbed to 10,000ft. Altitude was restricted on this first flight, because no cockpit pressurisation system had been installed, either. Then, after carrying out some preliminary manoeuvres to get the feel of the controls, he began his descent to rejoin the airfield circuit.

Suddenly, as Falk lowered the undercarriage on the downwind leg, Woodford Flying Control came on the R/T with an urgent warning that something had come adrift from beneath the 698. There was no indication in the cockpit that anything had gone wrong, so Falk continued to orbit the airfield and asked for another aircraft to be sent up to inspect the 698's underside. After some minutes a Vampire and one of the 707s joined him, and their pilots reported that the fairing panels behind both main

Above: VX777, the second prototype Avro 698, spent all its life as a ministry test and evaluation aircraft, ending its days at RAE Farnborough as an engineering/structures demolition job in 1963./ *RAE*

Below: Vulcan SR2 XH534 of No 27 Squadron displays its 'Dumbo' fin badge./*MoD*

undercarriage legs had broken off. There was no danger to the aircraft and Falk joined the circuit again, bringing the 698 down for a smooth landing that was shortened by the use of the brake parachute.

On 1 September, after two more short flights, the 698 flew to Boscombe Down, and during the week that followed appeared at the Farnborough Air Show on five occasions, and although security restrictions forbade a landing there, the crowds who witnessed the great white delta were left in no doubt about its manoeuvrability. The 698 was accompanied to the Show by the all-blue Type 707B, VX790, and the all-red 707A, WD280.

As soon as its participation at Farnborough was

Above left: The *Tirpitz* bulkhead, symbolising the rivalry between the V-force squadrons, with the No 9 Squadron team who finally 'rescued' it back from No 617 Squadron. Wg Cdr Ron Dick, the No 9 Squadron CO, is on the right shaking hands with Flt Lt Peter Armstrong./*RAF*

The last Vulcan B1 flying, XA903 was used for engine development from January 1964. *Above:* Here it is seen fitted with the Olympus 593 engine as used in Concorde and (*below*) it is seen arriving at RAE Farnborough on 23 February 1979 on its last flight, fitted with the Tornado MRCA's RB199 engine./*MoD; Bristol Sideley*

Above right: Vulcan B2 XM572 landing at Akrotiri with air brakes deployed ./*Rolls-Royce*

Far right: In 1972 a No 9 Squadron team flew from Akrotiri to Ohakea on a long range exercise. Their Vulcan was well and truly 'zapped', as the saying goes, by some crafty middle-of-the-night paintwork which can be seen over the head of slightly bewildered Chief Tech Pearsey./*RNZAF*

over, VX770 was grounded for modifications to the instrument panel and other changes that included a seat for the second pilot. It was flying again by the end of October and continued the test programme until May 1953, when it was grounded once more to be fitted with 7,500lb st Armstrong Siddeley Sapphire 6 engines. The Olympus was still not operational, although it had been tested in the Vulcan engine rig and had flown in a Canberra. The engine was, however, ready in time to be installed in the second prototype Vulcan, VX777, which flew for the first time on 3 September 1953 and appeared at Farnborough a few days later, accompanied by VX770 and all four Avro 707s (in red, orange, blue and silver).

The installation of the new engines in the second prototype meant that a lot of extra development work had to be carried out. The aircraft's pressurisation and radar systems also had to be fully tested at this stage, because it was intended to use VX777 for high altitude handling trials and navigation/bombing radar trials. VX777, incidentally, was the first Vulcan to have a visual bombing 'blister' under the nose. All these plans received a severe setback when, on 27 July 1954, VX777 was badly damaged in a heavy landing at Farnborough, leaving VX770 to carry on the development programme alone until its sister aircraft could be repaired. The accident caused serious delays in the engine development programme, but some of the programmed high altitude trials were carried out

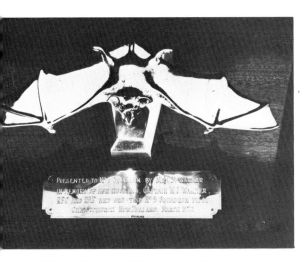

Left: The No 9 Squadron Vulcan arriving at Ohakea with an escort of RNZAF Skyhawks of No 75 Squadron./*RNZAF*

Below left: Vulcan B2As of the Waddington Wing at Nellis AFB for Exercise 'Red Flag'./*RAF*

Above: While in New Zealand the No 9 Squadron representatives were presented with a trophy depicting a bat – the squadron crest – by the widow of an earlier member of the squadron./*RNZAF*

by VX770, the aircraft being pushed to its maximum speed. Some quite severe buffeting was registered at speeds of Mach 0.80 to 0.85, and it was calculated that this could lead to fatigue in the outer wings. However, trials already carried out with wind-tunnel models indicated that the buffet threshold could be pushed back substantially by redesigning the outer wing, and the Phase 2 Wing, as it was known, was devised so that the outer leading edge, from 48.5% semi-span to the tip, was extended forwards by the addition of a new and thinner, downward-drooped leading edge.

The result was a wing that swept sharply at 52 degrees to 48.5% semi-span, 10 degrees less sharply to 78% and then at 52 degrees once more to a somewhat broader tip, producing a pronounced 'kinked' effect. The new wing was tested on Avro 707A WD280 and then, on 5 October 1955, on the second prototype Vulcan, after which it was approved for all production aircraft. Unfortunately, by that time it was too late to introduce it on the first few production machines, which were then flying or about to be rolled out.

The first production Vulcan B1, XA889, flew for the first time on 4 February 1955, finished silver overall (except for the new glass-fibre radome, which was black) and powered by four new two-spool Olympus 101 engines rated at 11,000lb st. The second

production aircraft, XA890, appeared at Farnborough that year and was upward-rolled before the crowds by Roly Falk, clearly demonstrating the big aircraft's remarkable manoeuvrability. Flight testing, meanwhile, continued with the two prototypes, VX777 having rejoined the programme in February.

As was the custom, a team of RAF personnel had worked alongside the Avro team during the Vulcan test programme. It was led by Sqn Ldr Charles C. Calder, who first flew the delta with Roly Falk on 18 February 1953. Towards the end of World War 2, while serving with No 617 Squadron, he had become one of the handful of pilots to drop the 22,000lb 'Grand Slam' bomb. By the end of 1955 a considerable nucleus of RAF crews had received experience on the Vulcan, and more followed when the first production aircraft, XA889, was delivered to Boscombe Down for Service acceptance trials in March 1956. By that time, other Vulcans were being delivered to the various Ministry of Supply establishments to play their part in the acceptance programme, XA890 undergoing radio and radar trials, XA891 being assigned to engine and fuel systems testing, and XA892 being allocated to armament trials. As a result of these tests, initial CA clearance for the Vulcan B1 was granted on 29 May 1956.

Royal Air Force crews, coming fresh to the Vulcan from the twin-jet Canberra, found a number of surprises in store. The first was the immense wing area and the general height of the aircraft from the ground – at least 6ft. Moving rearwards from the nose, past the bomb aimer's blister, one came to the entrance door, with the stalky, twin-wheel nosewheel assembly just behind it – causing some misgivings at first sight among navigators and AEOs, who felt that they might have trouble in abandoning the aircraft if the wheels were down.

Moving further back under the 3,550sq ft of wing, the next eye-catcher was the main undercarriage, built by Dowty, each leg having eight wheels on a levered-suspension bogie carried on a big magnesium alloy casting. The wheel wells also contained the refuelling and defuelling panels. The fuselage fuel bay was located immediately aft of the pressure cabin, and behind this was the 29ft weapons bay, large enough to accommodate the first nuclear weapons to enter service with the RAF. Alternatively, it could house 21 1,000lb conventional bombs in three clutches of seven. The weapons bay, because of its height above the ground, had to be loaded from trolleys by hydraulic jacks working directly on the bomb beams.

The crew of the Vulcan entered the pressure cabin via the underside door, which swung down to an angle of 45 degrees and had a ladder inside, one section of which slid down to hang vertically from the door's lower edge. Inside the cabin, just above and aft of the door, the two navigators and the AEO sat on bucket seats in line abreast on a raised platform, facing rearwards towards their equipment consoles. The two pilots climbed another ladder to the flight deck, squeezing between the two ejection seats (with some difficulty, if the men were on the large side) to take their places. The cockpit was well laid out, with full dual controls; the control columns were of the type usually associated with fighter aircraft, having pistol grips instead of the more normal 'spectacles', and the throttles were centrally placed between the pilots. The throttle quadrant also housed the four fuel gauges, airbrake switches and the parking brake lever. The engine instrument panel was directly above it, with the pilots' blind flying panels on either side. There were no controls or instruments on the cockpit roof.

The captain's console on the port side of the cockpit incorporated the radio, engine starting, bomb door and power flying control panels, while on the opposite side the second pilot was responsible for pressurisation, de-icing and air conditioning. The only real criticism of the cockpit was its restricted view; because the canopy was completely opaque there was no vision overhead or to the rear, the blankness being broken only by two small circular side panels. Through these, by leaning as far forward as possible and turning his head, the pilot could just see the wingtips. The view forward was also restricted by the position of the cockpit coaming, the angle at which the big delta 'sat' on the ground and the height of the cockpit, which could on occasions make marshalling a tricky procedure, especially in rain. It also created a problem when checking the correct function of the power controls, because the pilot was unable to see them. The usual procedure, after engine start, was for the crew chief – standing outside the aircraft, with his intercom plugged in – to confirm their operation, and as an added check the pilot had a visual indicator on the engine control panel. This was rather like an artificial horizon, with the addition of a tailfin and moveable indicators on the wings to represent the flying control surfaces.

Taxying was relatively uncomplicated. Once the aircraft was moving, it would continue to roll to the take-off point at idling RPM and the nosewheel was fully steerable, its operation controlled by a spring-loaded push-button on each control column. The take-off checks were also simple, and once they were completed the Vulcan was lined up on the runway and the engines opened up to full power while the pilots maintained pressure on the toe brakes. The nosewheel was used to steer the bomber until the

Above: The 'opposition' during 'Red Flag' – 'Soviet' RF-84 Thunderflashes.

Right: Victor K2 XL231 of No 57 Squadron leaving Greenham Common where it had been on static exhibition at the 1979 International Air Tattoo.
/Chris Cusack

rudder began to bite at around 60kts, the stick then being held forward to keep the nosewheel on the ground until unstick speed was reached. A slight backward pressure was then enough to lift the aircraft off the ground.

Apart from its high degree of manoeuvrability and its rate of climb, which was quite exceptional for an aircraft of its size in the mid-1950s, another remarkable quality about the Vulcan was its rate of descent. In a maximum-rate descent, the bomber could lose 20,000ft in 90sec flat, recovery to level flight being established in only about 1,500ft.

Their experiences with the Vulcan left the RAF Handling Squadron crews at Boscombe Down with the impression that the introduction of the bomber into squadron service would be an uncomplicated process, and that it would be well capable of carrying out the tasks assigned to it. No 230 OCU eagerly awaited delivery of its first aircraft, and during August 1956 Vulcan B1s XA895 and XA897 were allotted to it, although both aircraft were initially flown from Boscombe Down on Operational Reliability Trials. It was not until January 1957 that the OCU, at Waddington, near Lincoln, actually took two Vulcans on its inventory, and these were XA895 and XA898 – for in the meantime, XA897 had been the object of both triumph and tragedy.

In Service

On 9 September 1956, Vulcan XA897, one of the two B1s which had been allotted to No 230 Operational Conversion Unit and which had not completed its operational reliability trials at the A&AEE, Boscombe Down, took off from that airfield on the first leg of a goodwill flight to New Zealand via Aden, Singapore and Melbourne. The following month, while approaching to land in low cloud and rain at London Airport at the very end of what had been a triumphant tour, it struck the ground short of the runway, rose into the air again, but was so damaged as to be uncontrollable and crashed. The pilot, Sqn Ldr Howard, and the co-pilot, Air Marshal Sir Harry Broadhurst – at that time the Air Officer Commanding Bomber Command – escaped by using their ejection seats after making futile efforts to regain control; but the two navigators, the air electronics officer and an Avro representative in the rear of the crew compartment lost their lives.

The other Vulcan B1, XA895, became available to No 230 OCU in January 1957, and conversion training started the following month. Five more Vulcans were added to the OCU's establishment between then and 20 May, when the first OCU course qualified. This course immediately formed A Flight of No 83 Squadron, which, following two years' disbandment since operating piston-engined Avro Lincolns, now became the first RAF squadron to operate the Vulcan. For a short time the squadron used borrowed OCU aircraft, but on 11 July 1957 it received the first of its own Vulcans, XA905, and nine more aircraft were added to its inventory by the end of September. The great delta-winged bombers, distinctive in overall white anti-radiation paint, with the red cross of the City of Lincoln emblazoned on their fins and the squadron badge on their fuselage sides aft of the roundel, soon became a familiar sight over the Lincolnshire countryside as No 83 embarked on an intensive working-up period.

The skies of Yorkshire, too, were soon to tremble with the thunder of Bristol Olympus 102 engines, for on 15 October 1957 No 101 Squadron (a former Binbrook-based Canberra B6 unit, which had disbanded nine months earlier) was re-formed at Finningley, near Doncaster, and became the second front-line unit to operate the Vulcan B1. Its first Vulcan, XA909, arrived at Finningley two days later,

and by the end of the year No 101 had four aircraft on strength. Seven more Vulcans, all part of a new batch of 20 which had been ordered in 1954, were delivered to Nos 83 and 101 Squadrons before the end of April 1958, beginning with XH475; these aircraft were fitted with uprated Olympus 104 engines of 13,500lb st.

Nos 83 and 101 Squadrons both had distinguished operational careers during World War 2. Now, on 1 May 1958, they were joined in their V-Force role by another celebrated wartime RAF bomber unit: No 617 Squadron, the famous 'Dam Busters'. Re-formed at its original home, Scampton, near Lincoln, the base from which Wg Cdr Guy Gibson had led his Lancasters to breach the Ruhr Dams in May 1943, No

617 received eight Vulcan B1s, the first of which was XH482.

By this time, the crews of the first Vulcan squadron, No 83, had amassed a considerable amount of experience on the new type and were achieving consistently good results in bombing and navigation exercises. In October 1957, two of No 83's Vulcans took part in the USAF's annual Strategic Air Command bombing competition, and now, in 1958, the squadron was selected to carry out a series of goodwill tours overseas. The first of these took place in March, when two Vulcans flew to Nairobi for the official opening of Embakasi Airport. The first leg of the flight, to Wheelus Air Force Base, Tripoli, was accomplished in three hours, and the second, across

Left: Burnt out wreckage of Vulcan B2 XL385 at Scampton following an explosion in No 1 engine in the evening of 6 April 1967. The five-man crew and a 17-year old air cadet escaped. The Vulcan was carrying a Blue Steel training round./*RAF*

Top: Vulcan B2 landing at Waddington./*RAF*

Below: Probably the only Vulcan ever to bear an official name was B1 *Mayflower III* seen here arriving at Hanscom Air Force Base, Massachusetts. This No 9 Squadron aircraft, captained by Sqn Ldr Ron Dick, carried messages of greeting from the Mayor of the City of Lincoln on the anniversary of the sailing of the original *Mayflower*. /*RAF*

Above and below right: A full salvo of 21 1,000lb bombs falls away from a Vulcan and explodes in the sea during a live bombing sortie. /*RAF*

Overleaf, left: Vulcan B2 XM597 seen at Greenham Common. XM597 was the first Vulcan to carry the fin top radar warning receiver modification. Finished in gloss paint, it carries the older style red/white/blue roundels and fin flash./*Denis Calvert*

Overleaf, right: In contrast to XM597 this Vulcan B2 – XM607 of No 44 Squadron from RAF Waddington – has the later style matt finish camouflage paint with low visibility red/blue roundels and fin flashes./*Martin Horseman*

the Sahara to Entebbe, took 4hr 55min. After giving a display in front of an estimated 30,000 spectators at Embakasi, one of the Vulcans – XA904 – flew back to the UK, while the other, XA908, flew to Salisbury in what was then Southern Rhodesia, covering the 1,075 nautical miles from Nairobi in 2hr 15min. This Vulcan later returned home via El Adem.

A few weeks later, two more of No 83 Squadron's Vulcans flew to Buenos Aires as part of a British delegation to mark the Argentine Presidential Inauguration ceremonies, and afterwards went on to Rio de Janeiro for an official visit to Brazil. On both these overseas trips, AVM G. A. Walker, the AOC No 1 Group Bomber Command, flew as co-pilot in one of the Vulcans. Sadly, Vulcan XA908, which had made the African tour, crashed in Detroit during a visit to the United States on 24 October 1958, following complete electrical failure while en route to Lincoln, Nebraska. Another, fortunately less serious, mishap occurred almost exactly a year later, during a goodwill visit by XH498 of No 617 Squadron to New Zealand in October 1959; while attempting a landing at Rongotai (Wellington Airport) XH498 undershot slightly, sustaining damage to the port undercarriage and a port fuel tank, but the captain managed to overshoot and fly the aircraft to RNZAF Station Ohakea where he carried out a successful emergency landing. The Vulcan was repaired at Ohakea and flown back to Scampton in June 1960.

Meanwhile, as the three Vulcan B1 squadrons gradually assumed the role of spearhead of the British nuclear deterrent in 1958-59, other B1s had been allocated to the development programme of a more powerful version, the B2. The first of these was VX777, which was used to test the modified Vulcan wing planform and carried out many aerodynamic trials over a period of 3½ years before being flown to Farnborough for runway experiments in April 1960. It was scrapped in July 1963. Another B1, XA891, was re-engined with 16,000lb st Olympus 200s, and served as a test-bed until it was totally destroyed in a crash on the Yorkshire moors on 24 July 1959. The B2's electrics were tested in XA893, which was subsequently scrapped at Boscombe Down, while XA903 was modified for firing trials of the Blue Steel air-to-surface missile over the Woomera range in Australia.

The concept of the more powerful Vulcan B2 dated back to the middle of 1955, when Avro's Project Department came to the conclusion that the existing Vulcan Mk 1 airframe was capable of considerable further development, with particular regard to the installation of new engines, electronics and weaponry. The first task was to create yet another change in the wing planform which, in conjunction with increased power, would provide increased g

values, extra lift and an improved high-altitude performance. Design of the advanced Vulcan, the Mk 2, was therefore initiated in November 1955, and conversion of Vulcan B1 VX777 (the second prototype) as the prototype Mk 2 was begun in August the following year, a production order having been placed by the Air Ministry in June.

The first pre-production Vulcan B2, XH533, flew for the first time at Woodford on 19 August 1958, powered by Olympus Series 200 engines. The second B2, XH534, flew in 1959, powered by 17,000lb st Olympus 201 engines; this was the first aircraft to be fitted with a bulged tail-cone housing ECM equipment and tail-warning radar, a feature that was to become standard on all subsequent Vulcans. The first production B2, XH536, was demonstrated at the 1959 SBAC Show, XH534 being fully committed to Service Acceptance Trials at Boscombe Down, and the new mark was cleared for entry into service in May 1960. The first example of the Vulcan B2 to be delivered to No 230 OCU, XH558, arrived at Waddington on 1 July that year.

When deliveries of the Vulcan B2 began in July 1960, 34 B1s still remained in service, distributed between Nos 83, 101 and 617 Squadrons and No 230 OCU. The majority of the Mk 1s were subsequently withdrawn for conversion to Mk 1A standard, which involved the fitting of an extended tail cone and more advance electronics, including the provision of an electronic countermeasures aerial between the two starboard jet pipes. Most B1A conversions were carried out by Armstrong Whitworth, and the first of them – XH505 – rejoined No 617 Squadron in November 1960. Conversion work went on until March 1963, when Vulcan B1A XH503 returned to the Waddington Wing.

The first squadron to become fully operational with the Vulcan B2 was No 83; as its crews returned from conversion with No 230 OCU, its eight B1s were turned over to the newly-formed No 44 Squadron at Waddington from 10 August 1960. These were progressively converted to B1A standard, the first being XA904 which the squadron received in January 1961. This aircraft crashed on a night landing at Waddington on 1 March, and after repair became an instructional airframe. No 83 Squadron, meanwhile, had moved to Scampton in October 1960, and received its first B2, XH563, in December.

In the meantime, firing trials with test rounds of the Blue Steel ASM had been carried out in September 1960 from Vulcan B2 XH539, while two more Vulcan B2s, XH537 and XH538, were standing by to undergo trials with the Douglas XGAM-87A Skybolt missile, on which hopes for extending the life of the V-Force as the main British nuclear deterrent were then centred. In January 1961, Vulcan B2 XH563 of No 83

Squadron flew to the Douglas test field at Santa Monica, California, for electrical compatibility trials, and then went on for further tests to the Wright Air Development Division at Wright-Patterson Air Force Base, Ohio. The following November, XH537 flew for the first time from Woodford with two dummy Skybolt rounds installed on underwing pylons for aerodynamic tests, while XH538 carried out dropping trials, also with dummy rounds. Joint work on the application of Skybolt to the V-Force continued between Avro and Douglas throughout 1962, until the axe fell in December and the highly promising missile was cancelled. From that moment on, the days of the RAF's strategic deterrent force were numbered, and before the end of the decade the V-Force's primary role was to be taken over by Polaris-equipped nuclear submarines.

Meanwhile, Vulcan development was being stretched to its absolute limit. In May 1961, Vulcan B2 XH557 flew from Patchway with two 17,000lb st Olympus 201 engines in the inboard nacelles and two 20,000lb st Olympus 301s outboard; the latter engines were to become standard in late production Mk 2s,

Above: Vulcan B2 on final approach at Waddington into a strong crosswind./*RAF*

Bottom: Vulcan B2A XM646 landing at Waddington. the aircraft carries the badge of No 9 Squadron. Note the passive ECM aerial on top of the fin./*RAF*

Overleaf, left: Two views of B2 XM597. *Above:* With air brakes deployed above and below the wing, XM597 pulls out from a low level flypast. *Below:* This photograph shows to good effect the enormous delta wing of the Vulcan and the multiple sweep angles of the B2's leading edge. Both: *Denis Calvert*

Overleaf, top right: Vulcan B2 XH562 of No 44 Squadron overshooting the airfield at RAF Waddington in May 1976. In the background can be seen a number of the Waddington Wing's Vulcan B2s at dispersal./*Martin Horseman*

Overleaf, bottom right: A good view of the crew hatch and ladder of the Vulcan, as crew members dismount from B2 XL426./*MoD*

together with other modifications such as updated ECM, and Vulcans so equipped were designated B2A. The prototype B2A, XH557, subsequently returned to RAF service, together with several other B2 development aircraft. The prototype B2, XH533,

ended its days at RAF St Athan, where it was scrapped in 1970.

The second squadron to equip with the Vulcan B2 was No 27, which (having disbanded as a Canberra squadron at the end of 1956) re-formed as part of the Scampton Wing alongside No 83 Squadron on 1 April 1961. Both squadrons sent aircraft to the United States in October to take part in Exercise 'Skyshield II', achieving impressive successes in their role as attackers with the use of ECM. From September 1961 No 617 Squadron also began to re-equip with Vulcan B2s, bringing the Scampton Wing up to strength; its four Mk 1s and five Mk 1As went to No 50 Squadron, which had re-formed at Waddington on 1 August. Meanwhile, in June, No 101 Squadron had also moved to Waddington from Finningley with its five Vulcan B1s and two B1As, while No 230 OCU moved from Waddington to Finningley with its two Vulcan flights, one equipped with B1s and the other with B2s. The beginning of 1962 consequently saw three Vulcan B1/1A squadrons based at Waddington, all of them tasked for the nuclear strike role with free-falling weapons.

By this time Vulcan B2 production was well under way, and in 1962 another B2 Wing was formed at Coningsby. The first squadron was No 9, which re-

Above: Vulcan B2 of the Waddington Wing in the sights of an RAAF Mirage fighter during exercises over Malaysia./*RAAF*

Above right: Vulcan B2 XL389 of No 617 Squadron seen in 1973 just before that year's RAF Strike Command's Bombing and Navigation Competition. Note 'Dambusters' badge on fin./*M. Horseman*

Right: Front fuselage details on a Vulcan B2, XM600; the aircraft carries the Panther's Head badge of No 1 Group, RAF Strike Command./*Martin Horseman*

formed in March 1962; it was joined by No 12 in July and by No 35 in December. Some of the new-production Vulcans, suitably modified, were allocated to No 617 Squadron, and this became the first fully operational Blue Steel unit in February 1963 after several months of service development trials. The other two Scampton Wing squadrons equipped with Blue Steel later that year . In a change of policy that took effect from mid-1963 the whole of the V-Force was retrained for the low-level penetration role, so the traditional light paintwork of the Vulcans was replaced by light grey/dark green camouflage. In the course of time the Vulcans also began to display

Above: Vulcan B2 XM646 at RAF Waddington in April 1973, one of the early aircraft to be repainted with low visibility red/blue roundels and fin flashes. Also discernible on the main gear doors are antipodean zaps – a Kiwi, left, and Kangaroo, right.
/Martin Horseman

Above left: This photograph of B2 XL320 shows well the camouflage pattern on the upper surfaces of the Vulcan. It is carrying the fin flash of No 230 Operational Conversion Unit based at RAF Scampton.
/MoD

Below left: In contrast, the white underside of a B2 with the undercarriage doors in the final stages of closure. This aircraft is one of RAF Strike Command Vulcan B2s which took part in the SAC Bombing Competition 'Giant Voice' held at Barksdale AFB, Louisiana in 1974. It is seen here turning sharply away from a flypast over the base during the flying display held after the event.
/Martin Horseman

new electronics 'bulges' such as the small black nose radome housing terrain-following equipment, the result of low-level trials with a Vulcan from Cyprus in 1966. During 1964 a centralised servicing scheme was introduced, which meant that individual aircraft gradually lost their squadron identities; squadron badges disappeared, but all the aircraft of the Waddington Wing retained the City of Lincoln fin badge.

The reappearance of No 9 Squadron in 1962, incidentally, awakened an old rivalry which had existed between it and No 617 Squadron since World War 2. In November 1944 both squadrons had taken part in the famous attack on the German battleship *Tirpitz* as she lay in a Norwegian fjord, and each squadron claimed that its bombs had sunk the enemy vessel. The rivalry was epitomised by the saga of the *Tirpitz* Bulkhead, a fragment of the battleship acquired by No 9 Squadron after the war and displayed proudly in the crew-room – except when No 617 Squadron paid a visit, when the Bulkhead would

disappear and magically reappear in *their* crew-room. The trophy went back and forth between the two squadrons for years, until it was finally rescued in a 'raid' by a team from No 9 and firmly cemented into the crew-room wall at Waddington.

The phasing-out of the Vulcan B1/1A began in 1964, when No 230 OCU relinquished its B1s. The first to go was XA896, which went to Hucknall in June for conversion as test-bed for the Bristol Siddeley BS100 vectored-thrust engine which was to have powered the Hawker Siddeley P1154 V/STOL Mach 2 strike fighter, but the Vulcan was only partially modified when the P1154 project was cancelled and it was later broken up. The OCU's four other B1s went to Halton, Cosford, Cranwell and Newton for use as instructional airframes, so that by the end of 1965 the Conversion Unit was equipped solely with B2s.

Of the other B1s and B1As, XH499 was withdrawn from Waddington and assigned to Boscombe Down for specialised equipment trials; it was scrapped in November 1965. In March the following year, XH532 also left Waddington for No 19 Maintenace Unit at RAF St Athan; it was followed by 13 more B1As up to the middle of January 1968. After a short period in storage, all of them were scrapped. Ten more B1As continued to serve a little longer before being allocated for ground training to various airfields throughout the UK; the total included one which went to the museum at RAF Finningley and another which went to Akrotiri in Cyprus as a ground instructional airframe. After relinquishing their B1s and 1As, all three squadrons of the Waddington Wing converted to B2s.

Four other Vulcan B1s were assigned to engine development work, the first being the original prototype, VX770. This aircraft was delivered to Rolls-Royce at Langar in August 1956 and was fitted

with four 15,000lb st Conway RCo5 engines, beginning its trials on 9 August 1957. These included a visit to Malta, where tropical tests were carried out. After completing about 800 flying hours, VX770 was totally destroyed when it broke up during a 'Battle of Britain' air display at Syerston on 20 September 1958. Its place in the engine test programme was filled by XA902, which had been damaged in an accident at No 232 OCU in February that year. The aircraft was almost completely rebuilt and fitted with Conway 11 engines, which it tested for two years before being temporarily withdrawn and fitted with Rolls-Royce Speys in the inboard positions. It played a valuable part in the Spey test programme for several months between October 1961 and the middle of 1962, when it was withdrawn from use.

The third Vulcan B1 allocated to engine development was XA894, which went to Patchway in July 1960 and was converted as a test vehicle for the Bristol Olympus 22R, which was to power the ill-fated TSR2 tactical strike and reconnaissance aircraft. The engine was mounted in a ventral pod and

flight testing got under way in February 1962, but the aircraft caught fire during a ground run in December of that year and was totally destroyed after completing 78 hours' Olympus 22R testing. The replacement aircraft was XA903, which flew into Filton in January 1964. This Vulcan, which had carried out some 200 hours' flying in the Blue Steel development programme, was converted to take the Olympus 593, the powerplant developed for the Concorde supersonic transport. The conversion programme took two years and the first test flight was made on 9 September 1966. The Olympus 593 test programme occupied five years, at the end of which XA903 was withdrawn for a major overhaul and conversion as a test bed for the Rolls-Royce/Turbo Union RB199. With this unit mounted in a ventral pod, XA903 – the last Vulcan B1 to fly – carried out the first of a new series of test flights on 19 April 1973. It was a fitting close to the Vulcan Mk 1 story, for the RB199 was destined to power the Vulcan's successor in RAF service – the Tornado.

At the end of 1964, by which time the last Vulcan (XM657) had been delivered, Nos 9, 12 and 35 Squadrons were moved from Coningsby to Cottesmore, where No 12 Squadron disbanded on 31 December 1967. Its Vulcans went to Waddington, where Nos 44, 50 and 101 Squadrons re-equipped with the B2 in January 1968. From the end of 1970 the Blue Steel ASM ceased to be operational and all Vulcan B2 squadrons reverted to a conventional free-fall bombing role, although they could still be tasked for strategic nuclear use if the situation demanded it.

Early in 1969, Nos 9 and 35 Squadrons left Cottesmore for Akrotiri in Cyprus, where, under the designation Near East Air Force Bomber Wing, their task was to provide a tactical bombing spearhead for the Central Treaty Organisation. The training profiles carried out by the two squadrons were varied,

with Vulcans detaching westwards to the UK and eastwards to Singapore; a typical local exercise might involve four hours' flying over a distance of some 2,000 miles, the aircraft carrying out low-level simulated attacks and fighter affiliation. Practice bombing and flare dropping was carried out over Episkopi Bay, where there was a local range. In addition, there were detachments to Masirah, Nairobi and Ethiopia, mainly to provide long-range navigational practice, although in the case of Ethiopia there were other reasons. The first was that efforts were being made to re-establish relations with the Ethiopian Air Force, with which there had been little contact since the RAF left Aden; the second was to establish the suitability of the great expanses of central Ethiopia for low-level training. On several occasions, Vulcans which visited Ethiopia had their bomb bays filled with presents for the many children, mostly polio victims, who were inmates of two Cheshire Homes (sanataria founded by Grp Capt Leonard Cheshire, VC) at Addis Ababa and Asmara.

The search for suitable long-range navigational routes took one of No 9 Squadron's Vulcans from Akrotiri to New Zealand in 1972. Captained by Wg Cdr (now Air Cdre) Ron Dick, the aircraft made the journey via Masirah, Gan, Tengah, Darwin and RAAF Richmond, near Sydney. Wg Cdr Dick and

Above: XM605, one of the fourth production batch of B2s built by Avro's at Woodford, showing the typical B2 characteristics – big wing, ECM tail and flight refuelling equipment – on landing approach to Biggin Hill during September 1964./*Peter Gilchrist*

Bottom: Fourth production B2 with Olympus engines, XH536 is seen landing at the 1959 SBAC display. Note lack of extended, ECM-equipped rear fuselage.
/*Peter Gilchrist*

Right: XM650, a Vulcan B2 of No 50 Squadron, at Finningly during the Queen's review of the RAF. Note distinctive camouflage scheme and slots in upper surfaces of wing for air brakes./*Peter Gilchrist*

Bottom right: XM595, a Vulcan B2, seen at Biggin Hill during September 1964. Crew door is emblazoned with the RAF Scampton badge along with squadron badges for Nos 27 (elephant), 83 (antlers) and 617 (lightning). The bulge of Blue Steel can be seen in the bomb bay./*Peter Gilchrist*

his crew encountered torrential rain at Darwin, and on taking off the Vulcan entered cloud at 200ft. The entire crossing of Australia, in fact, was made over thick cloud. From RAAF Richmond the Vulcan went on to RNZAF Ohakea, in New Zealand's North Island, making the crossing in 2hr 45min at high speed, high level cruise. During their eight-day stay in New Zealand – where they displayed the Vulcan at the 1972 New Zealand Air Show, Hamilton, and over several towns – the No 9 Squadron representatives accepted a silver model of a bat, the Squadron's

badge, from the widow of an officer who had served on the squadron in 1928-9 and who had subsequently retired to New Zealand. An excellent tour was marred only by some small snags on the way back, including the failure of the windscreen heating, which caused the windscreens to crack at high altitude.

In the summer of 1974, when Turkish forces invaded the northern part of Cyprus, Nos 9 and 35 Squadrons dispersed briefly, then flew intensively on a variety of operational tasks, the Vulcans – among other things – acting as airborne relay stations. As

part of a political move, the two squadrons left Cyprus in February 1975, returning to the UK.

Meanwhile, in March 1972, No 27 Squadron had disbanded and then re-formed on 1 November 1973 in the maritime radar reconnaissance role, its freshly-equipped Vulcans now being designated SR2s. No 230 OCU moved to Scampton, which at the end of 1979 it was sharing with Nos 27, 35 and 617, while the Waddington Wing comprised Nos 9, 50, 44 and 101 Squadrons. In 1977 and 1978, crews from all the above squadrons with the exception of No 27 accompanied a detachment of four Vulcans to the United States to take part in 'Red Flag', the air warfare exercise held under very realistic conditions over the Arizona desert. The Vulcans operated at night, and despite the fact that the ground was not ideal for terrain-following some good results were achieved, showing that the Vulcan still had the ability to penetrate sophisticated defence systems.

Nevertheless, the Vulcan B2 is fast approaching the end of its useful life, and it will be phased out from 1982 as squadrons re-equip with the Tornado. It will be the end of an era; for, barring unexpected developments sometime in the future, the Vulcan will be the last truly long-range strategic bomber to serve with the Royal Air Force.

The Victor

Development and Testing

By the time Handley Page's tender to specification B35/46 had been accepted in November 1947, the design of their HP80 prototype had been virtually finalised in the Cricklewood drawing office. A number of changes were made during the latter months of 1947, the most important of which was the provision of more fin area and the moving of the tailplane to the top of the fin. At that time the T-tail configuration was every bit as novel as the HP80's crescent wing, so to test both theories Handley Page sought and obtained Ministry of Supply approval to build a radio-controlled scale model with a 10ft wingspan. Designated HP87, this unfortunately crashed on its first flight at Farnborough and was totally destroyed. In the meantime, however, the Ministry of Supply had authorised the building of a manned jet-powered research aircraft to test the HP80's aerodynamic characteristics. Designed to specification E6/48, the type – which was about one-third the size of the HP80 – was unusual, quite apart from its design, in that it was the product of three different companies and carried three company designations. The job of building it was given to Blackburn Aircraft at Brough, in Yorkshire, who designated it YB2; its fuselage was basically that of a Supermarine 510, with some modifications, and Supermarine designated it the Type 521; while Handley Page, the designer, referred to it as the HP88.

The HP88, powered by a 5,100lb st Rolls-Royce Nene 102 turbojet, flew for the first time at Carnaby, near Bridlington, on 21 June 1951, with test pilot G. R. I. Parker at the controls. This aircraft (VX330) subsequently made some 30 flights from Carnaby but, unfortunately, broke up during a high-speed, low-level pass along the main runway at Stansted on 26 August, killing Handley Page test pilot D. J. P. Broomfield. The cause was later found to have been failure of the slab-type tailplane's servo control

system, producing severe pitching oscillations and subjecting the airframe to intolerable g forces.

In any case, even if the HP88 had carried out its full test programme it would have been too late for any resulting information to have been incorporated in the HP80 design, for two prototypes had been ordered in April 1949 and by the time the HP88 flew in the middle of 1951 the first of these was in an advanced stage of construction. Each aircraft was to be powered by four Armstrong Siddeley Sapphire 100 engines delivering 8,000lb st, and the second prototype of the Handley Page Hastings transport aircraft (TE583) was modified as a test bed with two Sapphires in the outboard engine installations, flying for the first time in this configuration on 13 November 1950.

Handley Page had entertained hopes that the first prototype HP80, WB771, would be flown in time to be demonstrated publicly at Farnborough in September 1952. Its first flight, however, was delayed by a number of technical setbacks, including the discovery that the CG was much too far aft – so far, in fact, that 1,000lb of lead ballast had to be housed in the radar scanner bay to counteract it. Then there was a serious fire in the hydraulic system to the rear of the flash bomb bay, in which an electrician lost his life – and to complicate matters still further, when the damage had been repaired and the prototype was virtually complete, the Ministry of Supply decided that Radlett aerodrome was not big enough to ensure an adequate safety margin for the HP80's maiden flight.

This meant that the prototype had to be dismantled and transported by road to Boscombe Down, a move made in the utmost secrecy in June 1952. Handley Page went to extraordinary lengths to ensure that the new bomber was shielded from prying eyes as it was towed by a heavy tractor along the London-Southampton road; a framework was built on the low-loader that carried it and a white sheet was draped over the whole assembly. The idea was to make it look like the hull of a boat, and the legend GELEYPANDHY (a mis-spelt anagram of Handley Page) SOUTHAMPTON was stencilled on the side.

It was soon clear that the aircraft would not be ready in time for Farnborough. In fact, it was not until Christmas Eve, 1952, that Handley Page's chief test pilot, Sqn Ldr H. G. Hazelden, taxied the all-silver HP80 on to the main runway at Boscombe Down,

Top right: VX330, the HP88 crescent-winged research aircraft used to test the HP80's (Handley Page's tender to specification B35/46) aerodynamic qualities./*Hawker Siddeley*

Right: WB771, the first prototype Victor, seen landing at the 1953 SBAC display. WB771 crashed at Cranfield on 14 July 1954 following structural failure of the tail during low level trials./*MoD*

with E. N. K. Bennett as his flight observer. The aircraft took off in less than 1,500ft (a quarter of the distance available at Radlett) and Hazelden took it on a low, wide circuit lasting 17 minutes before touching down effortlessly. It was during the landing, in fact, that the Victor displayed one of its finest handling characteristics: if set up properly on final approach it would practically land itself. When most aircraft entered the ground cushion in the round-out stage just prior to touchdown, the ground effect tended to destroy the downwash from the tailplane, causing a nose-down moment and making it necessary for the pilot to hold off with backward pressure on the control column; the Victor's high-set tailplane eliminated this effect almost entirely. Also, the aircraft's crescent wing configuration reduced downwash at the root and upwash at the tips, a characteristic of normal swept wings, and this produced a nose-up pitch that contributed towards a correct landing attitude.

The HP80's structure was every bit as remarkable as its aerodynamics, and incorporated many features which were radical departures from any previous techniques. The wing, basically, was of multi-spar construction with load-carrying skins forming multiple torsion boxes; the inner part of each wing

was of three-spar construction, with a four-spar structure outboard of the landing gear. The all-metal ailerons operated through Hobson electrically-actuated hydraulically-powered control units; there were hydraulically-operated Fowler flaps on the inboard trailing edges, with two-piece hydraulically-actuated leading edge flaps on each outer wing (these were later replaced by fixed 'drooped' leading edges). The wing itself was of sandwich construction, with a corrugated core of aluminium alloy sheet for the skin and components such as ribs and spar webs, resulting in considerable strength combined with weight saving. The wing box ran ahead of the engines, which were completely buried in the thick inboard sections of the wings; there was adequate room for the installation of larger and more powerful units, and less risk of damage to the wing box if an engine caught fire or a turbine disintegrated. Much use was made of spot welding in attaching the outer skin to the core of the wing, a very bold move on the part of Handley Page at that time.

The fuselage assembly comprised three major components: front, combined centre and rear, and tail cone. The front fuselage housed the pressure cabin, containing most of the operational equipment and the crew of five; as in the Valiant and the Vulcan, the two pilots had ejection seats and the three rear members had swivel seats, facilitating their exit through a door in the port side of the cabin. Unlike the layout of the other two V-bombers, however, the Victor crew were not at markedly different levels; the two pilots, in fact, were seated very slightly lower than the three rear crew members. Later, a sixth seat was provided for the crew chief. Climbing into their ejection seats was far easier for the pilots than was the case with the Valiant or Vulcan, as they did not have to negotiate a central console; in the Victor, this could be pushed forwards and up towards the main panel, locking down into position when the pilots were seated.

The main fuselage section was taken up almost entirely by the enormous weapons bay, which was almost twice as large as that of the Vulcan – an advantage made possible by the crescent wing structure, which permitted the box-section fuselage joint to be set well forward. The bomb bay was completely unobstructed, its roof supported by four fore-and-aft girders which were attached to box-section frames providing the main supports for the bombs. As an alternative to the projected 10,000lb nuclear store, the aircraft could carry 35 conventional 1,000lb bombs. The bomb doors retracted into the fuselage in operation.

The fuselage centre section was joined to the rear section by a bulkhead which was specially stressed to accept tail loads. The rear section housed an equipment bay, tail radar, large hydraulically-operated air brakes and the base structure of the T-tail unit. Like the wings, this was a cantilever all-metal structure with corrugated sandwich skin panels.

Finally, the landing gear, designed by Electro-Hydraulics, consisted of two main units, each with eight-wheel bogies on an oleo-pneumatic shock absorber and retracting forwards; and the nosewheel, a twin-wheel assembly with hydraulic steering, retracting backwards.

By the time the prototype HP80 made its first flight Handley Page had received an order (dated 14 August 1952) for 25 production aircraft. Some of the delays of the previous year had now been offset by a relatively trouble-free flight test programme, which was proceeding on schedule. The only real snag occurred during the aircraft's fourth flight, when the main undercarriage tyres burst following a landing with brakes on. On 25 February 1953 WB771 was flown to Radlett, which was now to be its base

Left: Victors of Nos 55 and 57 Squadrons on QRA at Honington in the all-white anti-flash colour scheme./*John Hardy*

Below: XL511, one of the first Victor B2s to serve at Wittering. This aircraft was later converted to K2 standard in the tanker role.

following extensions to the main runway, and the only other significant setback that occurred during the next few weeks came in April, when as the result of a heavy landing the port main undercarriage bogies jammed in the vertical position. Fortunately, the only damage was again to the tyres and WB771 was soon in the air once more, flying up to four sorties a day. By the end of June it had cleared handling and systems and had also carried out many other trials, some involving crew escape.

At the end of August 1953, WB771 went into the Radlett paint shop and emerged with a new matt black finish, with silver-grey wings and full-length red flash – a colour scheme that gave it a somewhat evil and aggressive appearance. The prototype – named Victor in December 1952 – had already made its first public appearance, during the Coronation Review flypast of the RAF at Odiham on 15 July 1953, when it cruised past the Royal spectators at a modest 288kts; then, in September, it finally appeared at Farnborough alongside its rival, the Vulcan.

Much of the test programmes in November and December 1953 was occupied with trials of braking parachutes, a maximum of four being deployed; trials were also carried out with drogue parachutes fitted to the jettisonable cockpit roof, the idea being that these would lift the roof clear of the tail unit when it was 'blown'. The only hitch during the late 1953 series of trials came on the last day of the year, when WB771's

port inner flap fell off during a low speed run. The crew remained unaware of the occurrence until the aircraft landed.

February 1954 saw the Victor engaged in high-speed manoeuvring trials at high altitude. The flight crews reported that the aircraft handled well in steep turns at speeds of up to Mach 0.895.

Trials so far, however, had revealed the need for some structural modifications, including some to the tailplane. So that the flight test programme might proceed with the minimum delay, the tailplane from the second prototype, which was still under construction, was fitted to WB771 in place of its original one, and the programme was soon resumed.

On 14 July 1954, WB771 was carrying out a test programme that involved a series of high-speed, low-level runs over the aerodrome at Cranfield to carry out ASI position error checks. On one run the horizontal tail assembly started to flutter, then the

Below: Servicing a Victor B2 at RAF Wittering. The aircraft has a Blue Steel underslung.

Right: Victor K2 XL164 of No 57 Squadron refuelling Buccaneer strike aircraft of No 12 Squadron./*MoD*

Below right: Flanking a Hawker Hart biplane, two representative aircraft of the V-force, a Victor and Valiant, are pictured at Honington on the occasion of the presentation of the Queen's Standard to Nos 55 and 57 Squadrons on 20 July 1962. The Valiant was, in fact, a No 90 Squadron aircraft./*John Hardy*

Above left: Victor K2 XH673 of No 57 Squadron refuels a Harrier. /*MoD*

Left and above: Victor K2s XL164 and XL191 refuelling over the North Sea. Both tankers come from RAF Marham (Nos 57 and 55 Squadrons)./*MoD*

tailplane and elevators broke away and the Victor dived into the ground, impacting on the runway intersection. The crew were killed and the aircraft was destroyed. The cause was later attributed to fatigue failure of the three bolts which joined the tailplane to the fin.

At the time of the crash, WB771 had flown just under 100 hours. However, although its loss meant that the test programme came to a temporary standstill, there was no question of accelerating work on the second prototype, caution being the watchword. The second Victor, WB775, eventually took to the air on 11 September 1954, and after a 57min maiden flight appeared at Farnborough that same afternoon, with Sqn Ldr Hazelden once again at the controls. This aircraft was originally finished in the same black/silver grey colour scheme as WB771, but this was later changed to blue overall.

After carrying out handling trials at Radlett and Boscombe Down, WB775 was given a thorough overhaul and some modifications were made to its fin, including the fitting of a thicker skin. It was airborne again on 1 February 1955, and on the 3rd it began a series of trials involving the opening and closing of the weapons bay doors in flight. After a small number of sorties the aircraft was grounded while the flash bomb bay doors were sealed, as there was no longer a requirement for this installation. Modifications were also carried out to the bulkhead at the rear of the weapons bay, as tests with models had shown that the original configuration would have created a dangerous water trap, dragging down the Victor's nose in the event of a ditching.

On 14 March 1955 WB775 went to Boscombe Down for preliminary weapons trials with the A&AEE, and in June air drops were carried out over the Orfordness range. The second prototype Victor subsequently led a fairly routine life, testing a variety of systems until it was eventually dismantled at Radlett in 1959. Even then it continued to perform useful work, for its nose was used in water tank tests at the RAE, Farnborough.

Meanwhile, in 1955, the first production batch of Victor B1s was nearing completion. These aircraft differed from the prototypes in that they were fitted with 11,000lb st Armstrong Siddeley Sapphire 202

engines (ASSa7s); the nose was lengthened by 40in, partly to improve the CG range and partly so that the escape hatch would be further away from the port engine intakes. The original location of the hatch had caused some worries; trials had been carried out with the Sapphire Hastings, which had a replica Victor door built into its rear fuselage, and several live jumps – duly recorded on film – had been made from this aircraft, but the fact remained that the Hastings had a limiting speed of 175kts, and rear crew escape from the Victor at a substantially higher speed would have been hazardous. The production Victor B1 also had a number of other refinements, including the fitting of vortex generators on the wing and the removal of the dorsal fillet containing a combustion-heater intake, airframe de-icing now being handled by bleeding hot air from the engines. The height of the fin was reduced by 15in and it was broadened slightly, the tailplane being secured to it by four bolts.

The first production Victor B1, XA917, flew on 1 February 1956 and was retained by Handley Page for trials. The following year, on 1 June 1957, XA917 became the largest aircraft at that time to exceed the speed of sound, reaching Mach 1.1 in a shallow dive at 40,000ft. This was quite accidental, and it was a tribute to the Victor's aerodynamic qualities that the

crew had no warning other than the Machmeter indication that Mach 1 had been exceeded; the aircraft remained completely stable throughout and the control functions were perfectly normal.

The second production Victor B1, XA918, flew on 21 March 1956, and 10 production Victors were flying by the end of the year, engaged on trials work at Radlett and the various Ministry establishments. One of them, XA920, which had carried out general handling and performance trials, was flown inverted on one occasion while testing the camera installation intended for the photo-reconnaissance version of the Victor.

The first production Victors had all come off the assembly line painted a uniform matt silver, but in June 1956 one of the batch of 25, XA921, appeared in the new all-white anti-flash colour scheme. This aircraft subsequently carried out Service bombing trials, and in June 1959 it dropped a full load of 35 1,000lb bombs – the heaviest load ever released by a British bomber. Yet the Victor could do more: over short ranges, it could carry 39 2,000lb mines, representing a maximum overload weight of 78,000lb.

A few of the early Victor B1s spent the whole of their working life engaged on trials of one sort or another. XA917, the aircraft which had exceeded Mach unity, came to an untimely end when it was wrecked in a crash landing at Radlett; its cockpit section was installed at RAF Wittering, and later Wyton, for use as an emergency trainer. XA918 went on to become the prototype Victor K1 tanker conversion, while another of the early batch, XA919 – which had been rolled out a year behind schedule, having been used as a 'conference' airframe at Radlett – flew for the last time on 15 May 1961, when it went from Boscombe Down to Weston-Super-Mare airport and from there by road to RAF Locking, for use as an instructional airframe with No 1 Radio School. In September 1966 it went back by road to Handley Page, to end its days as a fatigue and structure development airframe in a ground rig. A more inglorious end awaited XA920, which flew to Stansted on 25 September 1963 and was then shipped to the mud-flats of Shoeburyness, for use in the armament trials work of the Proof and Experimental Establishment.

Left: Victor K2 of No 55 Squadron refuelling Lightnings of No 11 Squadron./*MoD*

Below: The first Victor K1, XA937, arriving at Marham, 1 February 1966./*RAF*

In Service

On 28 November 1957 No 232 Operational Conversion Unit received its first Victor B1, XA931, at Gaydon in Warwickshire. The first Victor OCU course qualified in April 1958 and the majority of its graduates went to the first Victor squadron, No 10 which received its first aircraft on 9 April and formed on the 15th. Other graduates of the course went to RAF Wyton to join the radar reconnaissance flight with two of the OCU's Victors. At the end of July 1958, following the completion of 1,000-hour intensive flying trials, fatigue cracks were discovered in a Victor tailplane, and in August all the OCU's Victors were grounded while their tailplanes were removed for repair.

The second Victor B1 squadron, No 15, formed at Cottesmore on 1 September 1958, and the third, No 57, at Honington on 1 January 1959, taking delivery of its aircraft (all late production B1s) from March. Two of the later batch of Victor B1s, in the meantime, had been assigned to trials work; one of them, XA930, had made a series of rocket-assisted take-offs from Radlett with two de Havilland Sprites fitted in jettisonable nacelles, and on 27 August 1958 it flew with auxiliary underwing fuel tanks and a prototype flight-refuelling probe installation. The other trials aircraft, XA933, was used for a time by 232 OCU on low-level radar development work, afterwards going to the A&AEE at Boscombe Down.

During 1959 the basic Victor B1 underwent several important changes; these included the provision of a flight refuelling probe, the fitting of drooped leading edges, tail-warning radar, new ECM equipment under the nose and in the rear fuselage, and the strengthening of the pressure cabin. This modified aircraft emerged as the Victor B1A and the first of this mark to be accepted on charge was XH613, 34th aircraft on the Victor production line, although it initially lacked a refuelling probe. The first B1As, fully converted, entered service with No 15 Squadron in July 1960, and over the months that followed the squadron's B1s were also modified to B1A standard. In September 1960 No 55 Squadron also formed at Honington with B1As, and its sister squadron, No 57, gradually updated its B1s to the new mark in 1961.

Meanwhile, work had been proceeding at Radlett on the design of the Victor B2, on which the Victor force was to standardise in the 1960s. The major design change was the installation of a new powerplant, the 17,250lb st Rolls-Royce Conway RCo11 engine, which would give the B2 the necessary altitude to survive in a hostile SAM environment and ultimately provide greater range for the developing air-to-surface missile role and also for strategic reconnaissance, where a combination of range and altitude was necessary for adequate coverage of potentially hostile areas.

Handley Page received a contract for 21 Victor 2s

in June 1956, and following extensive ground testing of the new engines the whole of the wing root area was redesigned, with the engine bays and intakes deepened and widened. Provision was also made for the installation of a Blackburn Artouste auxiliary power unit in the starboard wing root, so that the engines could be started independently of ground services. Retractable scoops, designed to feed air to the emergency turbo-alternators in the modified electrical system, were also fitted on the upper rear fuselage, and the root of the fin's leading edge was extended slightly to house a duct that supplied air to the rear glycol system. Victor B1As had a similar duct under the fuselage, but this was prone to clogging with 'Window' countermeasures foil.

The prototype Victor B2, XH668, flew for the first time on 20 February 1959, and was all set for delivery to Boscombe Down for service handling trials when, on 20 August, it failed to return from a sortie over the Irish Sea off Pembrokeshire. The loss of the aircraft

Below: The first Victor K2 arrives at Marham, 7 May 1974./*RAF*

Right: Victor K2 of No 57 Squadron from RAF Marham after making a precautionary landing on a foam strip at RAF Leeming, because of undercarriage problems./*MoD*

Below right: Arrival of the first Blue Steel Victor B2 at RAF Wittering for delivery to No 139 Squadron in August 1963.

was, at the time, a complete mystery, for the impact had not been registered on radar and there had been no radio transmission from the crew. A fleet of salvage vessels – 39 in all, including 27 chartered trawlers – was assembled and a lengthy operation began to dredge that part of the sea bed where the wreckage of the Victor was believed to be. By the end of the year, the ships had brought up 597,610 pieces of wreckage, nearly 70% of the aircraft, and the painstaking work of reconstruction began at RAE Farnborough. It was eventually established that the

cause of the accident had been the loss of a pitot tube, producing faulty ASI and Machmeter readings which led to the Victor exceeding its airframe limitations, going into an uncontrollable dive and breaking up.

The test programme continued with the next four B2s, XH669-XH672, and XH669 was displayed at Farnborough in September 1960. By this time the original Victor B2 order had been substantially reduced in the wake of a government defence review, when it was decided that the planned introduction of Skybolt, the American air-launched ballistic missile,

Left: Members of a No 100 Squadron team with bombing trophies. The large trophy, depicting an Eagle with outstretched wings, is the Minot Trophy, the premier award in the RAF Medium Bomber Force Bombing and Navigation Competition. It was also won by No 57 (Victor B1) Squadron in 1963.

Below left: A Victor SR2 of No 543 Squadron at RAF Wyton showing the extra wing section inboard of the engine intakes which is a distinctive feature of the Mk 2. This aircraft, XL165, was the prototype of the strategic reconnaissance version first flown in February 1965./*Martin Horseman*

Above and below: Victor K2 XM715 of No 55 Squadron, RAF Marham, landing on the grass after running out of asphalt at RAF St Mawgan on 5 August 1975 when arriving for the International Air Day./*F.J. Boreham*

meant that the V-Force required fewer aircraft. In September 1961 a Victor B2 trials unit, designated C Squadron of No 232 OCU, was formed at Cottesmore; aircraft allocated to it included XL188, the first B2 to be delivered to the RAF (on 2 November 1961), XL189 and XL165. Meanwhile, early production B2s had been going through their paces at Boscombe Down, some of them on Blue Steel trials.

On 1 February 1962 the first Victor B2 squadron, No 139 (Jamaica) Squadron, formed at Wittering with an initial strength of six Victor B2s. It was also planned to equip Nos 9, 12 and 100 Squadrons with Victors, and in April 1962 the Victor trials unit at Cottesmore was redesignated the Victor Training Flight, its function being to train B2 crews for the new squadrons. In the event, Nos 9 and 12 Squadrons were to re-equip with Vulcans, but on 1 May 1962 No 100 Squadron once again came into being, its Victors joining those of No 139 at Wittering.

By the end of 1962 these squadrons had 13 Victor B2s between them. Most of the other 17 B2s which

Left: Fin, rudder, tailplane and rear end details on a No 543 Squadron Victor SR2 at RAF Wyton; the unit badge featured a heron with a padlocked bill./*Martin Horseman*

had flown so far were engaged on trials or development work of one kind or another, much of this involving the modification of the aircraft to carry Blue Steel. Early trials with the weapon were in fact carried out by a Victor B1 in 1960, but towards the end of 1962 three B2s were allocated to the programme. Of these, XH674 was used to test the necessary systems, XL161 did live launches at Woomera and XL164 incorporated additional electronic equipment and certain design changes, including streamlined fairing pods known as 'Kuchemann carrots' (after Dr Dietrich Kuchemann, an aerodynamicist who joined the Royal Aircraft Establishment in 1946 and who became Head of the Aerodynamics Department in 1966) on the wing trailing edges, housing 'Window' dispensers. This aircraft, with all its modifications, was the first of a new breed of Victor, designated B2R by the company – the 'R' standing for Retrofit. The B2R incorporated drooped leading edges, which had been tested on XL159; the latter was lost when it spun and crashed during trials near Newark in March 1962.

The conversion of existing B2s to B2R standard continued throughout the spring and summer of 1963, the first of the modified aircraft being delivered to No 139 Squadron in August. No 139 therefore became the first of the Victor Blue Steel squadrons; by December 1963 it had received its seventh B2R, XL513, the first Victor to be camouflaged with dark green and brown upper surfaces (changed to dark grey/green soon afterwards) in connexion with the V-Force's new low-level role, and its existing B2s were shared out between No 100 Squadron, the Victor Training Flight (the latter having moved to Wittering in April 1963) and the Handley Page factory at Radlett, where they were progressively brought up to B2R standard. No 100 Squadron received the first of the retrofitted B2Rs in the middle of January 1964, becoming the second Victor Blue Steel squadron. Strictly speaking, all Victor B2Rs assigned to the Blue Steel role bore the Service designation B2BS, but in practice they were never referred to as anything other than B2s. On 1 March 1964 centralised servicing was introduced at Wittering, and from then on ground crews and technical personnel were directly responsible to the station's Technical Wing, the squadrons consisting of aircrew only.

February 1964 saw the disbandment of the original Victor squadron, No 10, to be followed by No 15

Squadron in October. The previous December, No 15, together with No 57 Squadron, had performed valuable service in the Far East, their Victors being detached to Singapore and Malaysia to provide a show of force during the confrontation with Indonesia, whose forces had been carrying out armed incursions into Malaysian territory. No 55 Squadron was also detached to this troubled area during 1964.

It had been planned that Victors would replace the Valiant in the tanker role, and conversion work was begun on a prototype Victor tanker in the spring of 1964. Conversion included the fitting of two fuel tanks in the bomb bay, a Flight Refuelling Mk 20B refuelling pod under each wing to supply high-speed tactical and fighter aircraft, and a Flight Refuelling Mk 17 hose-drum unit in the rear of the bomb bay to supply bombers and transport aircraft. The prototype tanker was XA918, the second production Victor B1, and after this aircraft had successfully completed its trials at Boscombe Down the Victors which had formerly belonged to Nos 10 and 15 Squadrons were converted at Radlett, the first conversion, XH620, flying on 28 April 1965. Work on the Victor tanker conversions was speeded up following the decision to phase out Valiants earlier than planned when fatigue cracks were discovered in the main wing spar; this decision precipitated something of a crisis, for although the Valiants involved no longer formed part of the strategic deterrent, having been assigned to NATO in a tactical role two years earlier, the Valiant tanker force formed an integral part of RAF operations, and its withdrawal from service created a dangerous gap.

Therefore, when the first Victor tanker, XH620, and four more Mk 1A two-point tankers were delivered to No 55 Squadron at Marham during May and June 1965, they were not full conversions, for they still retained their bombing capability and were fitted only with the Mk 20B underwing pods. They were, in fact, rushed into service as quickly as possible to provide flight refuelling support for the Lightning interceptor squadrons, for the demise of the Valiant at the beginning of 1965 had left the RAF without air-to-air refuelling facilities.

No 55 Squadron, which had relinquished its bombing role in March 1965, was fully operational in the tanker role in June of that year, and during the weeks that followed its Victor B(K)1As carried out a series of trials and refuelling exercises with the Lightnings of Nos 19 and 74 Squadrons, several involving trips to Malta and Cyprus. Meanwhile, work was proceeding at Radlett on the conversion of 10 Victor B1s as full three-point tankers; none of these retained a bombing capability and the first, XA937, flew on 2 November 1965 with the designation Victor K1. This aircraft subsequently went to Boscombe Down for radio trials, then like the others went to No 57 Squadron, which moved to Marham in December 1965 to convert to the tanker role. At a later date, three-point conversions were made from Victor B1As, the resulting tankers being designated K1As.

On 1 July 1966 No 214 Squadron, whose Valiants had pioneered operational flight refuelling techniques in the RAF, also re-formed at Marham and received its first Victor B(K)1s in September, completing the Marham Tanker Wing. No 55 Squadron re-equipped with Victor K1A three-point tankers early in 1967 and a Tanker Training Flight was also set up at Marham, flying a mixture of K1s and K1As. It was redesignated No 232 OCU in February 1970.

In the strategic deterrent role, meanwhile, the Victor had come to the end of its days. On 14 and 15 June 1968, six Victor B2s of Nos 100 and 139 Squadrons led a V-Force flypast at the Queen's Review, which took place at RAF Abingdon; it was their public finale, for on 1 October No 100 Squadron disbanded and No 139 followed suit on 31 December, their aircraft returning to Radlett – all except two, one of which (XL188) went to Boscombe Down and the other (XM717) to join the strategic reconnaissance fleet of No 543 Squadron at RAF Wyton, where it replaced XM715, which had been withdrawn from use after suffering damage to a wing the previous year.

The premature retirement of the Valiant B(PR)1 in January 1965 had led to the Victor being phased into the reconnaissance role somewhat earlier than planned, for the Valiant was to have remained in service until 1967. Work was accelerated on the prototype PR Victor, XL165, and this was flown at Radlett on 23 February 1965 with the designation Victor SR2, being deliverd to the A&AEE Boscombe Down for acceptance trials in March. The second SR2 conversion was XM718, which had been rebuilt following a crash landing at Wittering; this aircraft also went to Boscombe Down and was eventually delivered to No 543 Squadron in January 1966. The squadron's first SR2 was XL230, which was delivered to Wyton on 18 May 1965, the 11th and last SR2 arriving on 21 June 1966. Unfortunately, just a few days later, while carrying out a low-level demonstration for the benefit of Press photographers on 29 June, SR2 XM716 broke up in mid-air and crashed at Warboys with the loss of its crew.

The tasks undertaken by No 543 Squadron throughout its career were immensely varied. One of the most important was maritime radar reconnaissance; in a single seven-hour sortie a Victor SR2 could provide coverage, irrespective of cloud, of an area the size of the Mediterranean, pinpointing the position of any ship and tracking all submarine movements in that area. The Victors also carried out extensive photographic survey work on behalf of both the British and foreign governments. As far as the RAF was concerned, global mapping and geophysical survey assumed a new degree of importance with the advent of Blue Steel, whose inertial navigation system depended on accurate knowledge of where the missile was at the time of launch and also of the target's co-ordinates. The reconnaissance force came

Below: Shortly before the disbandment of No 543 Squadron, Victor SR2 XH674 stands ready to make one of the unit's last sorties on 21 May 1974./*Martin Horseman*

Top right: Victor SR2s at RAF Wyton in April 1973. /*Martin Horseman*

Centre right: Nose and cockpit area detail on a Victor SR2 showing the in-flight refuelling probe extending from the line of the upper fuselage./*Martin Horseman*

Bottom right: B1 XH 588 of No 15 Squadron during the 1960 SBAC display. This machine was modified to B1A standard and eventually flown by No 57 Squadron duting rotational detachments to RAF Tengah in Malaya./*Peter Gilchrist*

under the control of No 1 Group, as did the Joint Air Reconnaissance Intelligence Centre, which was responsible for the exploitation of reconnaissance material and the dissemination of the resulting information. No 543 Squadron disbanded on 24 May 1974, its maritime radar reconnaissance role having been taken over by the Vulcan SR2s of No 27 Squadron, which had re-formed the previous November.

During the late 1960s, meanwhile, the Victor Tanker Force had amassed considerable experience in its role of supporting the operations and deployments of the RAF's shorter range combat aircraft, both in the NATO area and world wide, a role that assumed greater importance as the RAF's permanent bases overseas gradually dwindled. A typical example was Exercise 'Ultimacy', which involved the deployment of Lightning fighters of No 5 Squadron to Tengah, Singapore, in December 1969. The first refuelling contact with the Victors was made over East Anglia in the darkness at 03.45hrs, the fighters then crossing France and the Mediterranean to make another rendezvous off Cyprus. After making a night stop at Masirah, the Lightnings set off

once more over 4,000 miles of Indian Ocean to Singapore, making another refuelling contact with Victors operating out of Gan island. The Lightnings remained at Tengah for a month, taking part in air defence exercises before returning to the UK. With such support from the Victor tankers, fighters from the UK could reach Cyprus in 4½ hours and the Arabian Gulf in eight; in 1970, refuelled by Victors of the Marham Wing, two Phantoms flew non-stop from London to Singapore in a world record time of 14hr 8min.

Operations with Victor K1 and K1A aircraft during the 1960s had revealed a requirement for a K2 variant, with a longer range, increased power and greater fuel uplift, especially when operating from airfields at high altitude in hot climates. Late in 1968, therefore, it was decided to convert either B2R XM175, which had sustained wing root damage and which was then in storage at Radlett, or XL614, which was at St Athan, to K2 standard for trials. These were to be followed by 28 other conversions, which were to include No 543 Squadron's Victor SR2 fleet. In the event, however, the SR2s were not modified to tanker configuration, and the

requirement for the K2 was reduced to 21 aircraft, some K1As being retained in service.

It was originally planned that the Victor K2s would enter service in 1973, but the conversion programme was subjected to serious delays by Handley Page's financial difficulties in 1969-70. Although Handley Page did all the design work for the conversions the company never actually received a contract; on 8 August 1969 the Official Receiver was called in and the firm became a subsidiary of the K.R. Cravens Corporation of St Louis, finally closing down in February 1970. Later in the year, a government contract for K2 conversion work passed to Hawker Siddeley Aviation, and the Victors – all surplus B2Rs – were transferred to Chadderton and Woodford, the former Avro factories where the Vulcan had been produced.

The first Victor K2 conversion to return to RAF service was XL233, which joined No 232 OCU on 7 May 1974. On 1 July the following year No 55 Squadron, commanded by Wg Cdr K. J. Lovett, became the first to equip with the more powerful aircraft, and later that year it assisted in the rapid deployment of Hawker Siddeley Harrier V/STOL strike aircraft to Belize, as well as carrying out refuelling trials with the Panavia Tornado. No 57 Squadron also re-equipped with Victor K2s from 7 June 1976, No 214 Squadron retaining its K1As until disbandment on 28 January 1977. This left Nos 55 and 57 as the RAF's only tanker squadrons, although at the time of writing (1980) the tanker force is scheduled to be supplemented by some converted VC10s.

Top left: B2 XL233 of No 100 Squadron at the 1964 SBAC display equipped with Blue Steel.
/Peter Gilchrist

Below left: XL164, a Victor B2, at the SBAC display of 1960 in standard antiflash white paint scheme. Note lack of refuelling probe.
/Peter Gilchrist

Top: XH591, a Victor B2, at Biggin Hill 1964; note refuelling probe. XH591 was later modified to K1A standard./*Peter Gilchrist*

Below: B2 XL164 landing at the 1960 SBAC display. This machine was used for development work./*Peter Gilchrist*

Blue Steel
and
Skybolt

Blue Steel

In 1954, following the issue of an Air Ministry Operational Requirement, both the Royal Aircraft Establishment and A. V. Roe initiated studies on the feasibility of a 'stand-off' bomb – in other words, one that could be released when the parent aircraft was still some distance away from the target – as a possible means of extending the effectiveness of the RAF's new generation of medium bombers. By the end of 1955 most of the major decisions about the missile's aerodynamics had been taken. The first was that it was to have a tail-first configuration, because this had a favourable centre of pressure change with Mach numbers; although the centre of pressure moved rearwards through the transonic regime it then moved forwards again, so that by careful design the static margin could be very nearly the same at both supersonic and subsonic speeds. This was a crucial point, for any instability during the launch phase could have had serious consequences for the parent aircraft. The wing planform – a 60-degree delta – was selected because it gave good performance at transonic speed and also at the low supersonic speed that would be attained when the missile climbed. A large wingspan, although this would have given an increase in altitude, was rejected because of the geometry of the aircraft that would be available to carry the weapon. The span of the foreplane, which was all-moving, was to be half that of the main wing. The missile was to have two fins, similar in planform to the main wing and the foreplane, but the lower fin was to be larger than the upper. Finalising the rest of the aerodynamic design occupied much of the next two years and involved an extensive wind tunnel programme to investigate the behaviour of the canard configuration at transonic and supersonic speeds, because when the design was initiated such data was practically non-existent. Nine models, ranging in scale from 1/6th to 1/48th, were built and subjected to wind tunnel tests.

In March 1956 Avro received a development contract. There were three other main contractors: Armstrong Siddeley for the propulsion rocket motors, Elliott Automation for the inertial navigation system (designed by the RAE), and de Havilland Engines for the power supply turbines and also for some of the special propulsion motors to be used in early test vehicles.

The wind tunnel programme was supplemented by a series of free flight trials using 1/8th scale models. These were ground launched, using tandem solid fuel rocket boosters of two types so that the subsequent decelerating glides could be assessed in both the transonic and supersonic speed ranges.

The guidance and control system developed for the missile – known by the codename 'Blue Steel' from 1956 – consisted of three parts: the inertial navigator, supplied by Elliotts, and the flight rules computer and autopilot, both supplied by Avro. The decision to incorporate an inertial navigation system in the weapon, taken in 1954, showed considerable forward thinking, for it was the only system that enabled a weapon of the Blue Steel type to navigate precisely without help from the ground and without sending out radar emissions. The general principle was that the inertial navigator computed the present position of the missile, the flight rules computer determined its flight plan, and the autopilot signalled the necessary control movements to obtain the required flight path. During the flight prior to release, the missile's navigation system was linked with that of the parent aircraft, providing additional information to the crew on their position and, by comparing data obtained from fixes along the route, enabling corrections to be fed into the missile. The navigation system also contained a homing computer which analysed information about the missile's present position and velocity and computed the steering signals that were necessary to bring Blue Steel to its target. The flight rules computer took information from both the present position computer and homing computer and used it to decide when the missile was to climb, to cruise and how it was to use its power, and during the final stage of the flight it connected the steering signals provided by the homing computer to the autopilot.

Airborne trials using 2/5th scale models of Blue Steel were started in 1957, using a Valiant aircraft (WP204) based at the Avro Weapons Research

Top right: Blue Steel nuclear 'stand-off' weapon which was powered by BS Stentor rocket motor, controlled by Elliot Inertial system driving moving foreplanes and elevons. Seen here at the 1964 SBAC display, its main disadvantage was its range – 100nm./*Peter Gilchrist*

Right: The Blue Steel servicing bay at Wittering.

Division, Woodford, the drops being made over the Aberporth range. These models were constructed of stainless steel, but manipulation of this proved difficult and a different type of steel was used in later vehicles. The models were powered by a solid fuel rocket motor and were carried inside the Valiant's bomb bay, being dropped like a normal free-fall missile. The motor fired a few seconds after launch and the autopilot took over, the missile then accelerating to moderate supersonic speed and performing programmed test manoeuvres during a

Loading and unloading Blue Steel was a complex procedure, requiring several different items of associated ground equipment. These photographs show the return of the last QRA Blue Steel to its hangar at RAF Wittering after the Victor force relinquished that role in 1968.

flight lasting several minutes. The flights were normally terminated by a built-in destruct system. The test programme with these models was completed in 1958, but a few more were launched in 1959 to give RAF aircrew preliminary training in the operation of the future full-scale missile.

Trials of full-size Blue Steel test vehicles began in 1958, by which time the Valiant had been joined by Vulcan Mk 1 XA903. The full-size vehicles were all originally intended to be constructed of stainless steel, but because of the time spent in learning manufacturing techniques and associated delays in starting the trials some of the test vehicles were made of aluminium alloy. The other main difference between the test vehicles and the operational Blue Steel was that the former were all powered by de Havilland Double Spectre rocket motors, whereas the operational version was to be fitted with the Armstrong (later Bristol) Siddeley Stentor. The first two aluminium alloy test vehicles were launched in 1958, both of them inert dummies, but several powered versions were launched in 1959 and 1960, both at Aberporth and at Woomera in Australia.

Trials with full-scale, stainless steel Stentor-powered Blue Steels were begun at Woomera in the summer of 1960, using Vulcan XA903. The Stentor rocket motor was a dual-chamber liquid propellant rocket engine, using kerosine as fuel and hydrogen peroxide as the oxidant. To start the engine, hydrogen peroxide was expelled from a starting tank by pressurised nitrogen and decomposed in a catalytic steam generator which supplied steam to the turbo-pumps. When the turbine reached a high speed, this supply of hydrogen peroxide was provided by the pumps which fed the combustion chamber. Each combustion chamber contained a catalyst pack, and hydrogen peroxide passing through this into the combustion zone was decomposed into a mixture of oxygen and superheated steam. Fuel injected into this mixture ignited spontaneously and the combustion products were accelerated during their passage through the expansion nozzle. On its way to the combustion zone, the hydrogen peroxide passed down to the end of the expansion nozzle and back to the top of the chamber through passages in the chamber wall, to act as a coolant during firing. Both combustion chambers fired while the missile was being boosted to supersonic speed, then the larger chamber was cut off by command from the flight rules computer. The smaller ran at full thrust for most of the climb, when it was throttled back for cruise by the flight rules computer.

Blue Steel was designed to be carried for several hours below an aircraft fuselage at high altitude, in temperatures as low as −70°C. Before launch, however, some of its internal equipment might be functioning for a considerable time, producing excess heat, while during the boost to supersonic speed its outer skin heated rapidly. Much consideration was therefore given to temperature control, and the problem was approached in three ways. First, a lot of the missile was double-skinned to slow down the ingress of heat during free flight and the loss of heat during carriage; second, a warm air supply produced from a heat exchanger was piped from the parent aircraft into the missile during carriage; and third, a freon refrigeration system installed partly in the aircraft and partly in the missile piped liquid freon into equipment systems which had the dual (and undesirable) property of being both heat producing and temperature sensitive.

One of the biggest problems which had to be surmounted was the marrying of Blue Steel to the aircraft that were to carry it operationally, the Vulcan B2 and Victor B2. The missile had to be compatible with both aircraft and special Blue Steel equipment had to be carried in them, involving a good deal of detail design. The interface between missile and aircraft was complex and included the aircraft structure, fairings, release mechanism, hydraulic power supplies, electrical control, warm air and refrigeration supplies, monitoring and data transfer and lanyard operating units, and every connection had to separate cleanly on missile release. The aircraft also required special controls for the missile navigation system and controls to monitor the function of the other missile systems, all of which meant fitting more instrumentation into already crowded cockpits.

The first firing tests of Blue Steel in Australia, from Vulcan B2 XH539, took place at Woomera early in 1961, and at a later date a Victor B2 also joined the trials programme, compatability tests having been carried out in 1960 with a Victor B1; three B2s were allocated (XH674, XL161 and XL164) and it was XL161 which carried out live drops of the missile at Woomera. One of the problems of compatibility with the Victor lay in the small ground clearance of the latter's bomb bay, and Blue Steels designated to equip the Victor squadrons had a special modification in the form of a folding upper fin. With the Vulcan, whose weapons bay was six feet above the ground, the problem was exactly the opposite, and different designs of low loader were prepared to suit each aircraft type, one loader operating mechanically and the other hydraulically. The latter was subsequently adopted as standard and was fitted with height adaptors to compensate for the different ground clearances of the two V-bombers. Other special ground equipment included an airfield transporter trolley; the missile was filled with propellant while on this and then taken from the preparation building to the low loader, in position beside the aircraft. The transporter trolley carried equipment to monitor the kerosine and peroxide, which were kept under constant surveillance.

To train aircrew in the operation of Blue Steel's navigation and monitoring systems, Avro produced a special trainer version of the missile. The configuration was the same as that of the operational weapon and the trainer was attached to the aircraft in the same way, but it had no rocket motor, propellant or warhead and was not designed to be released in flight. These trainers were installed at the Bomber Command Bombing School, RAF Lindholme, where Vulcan B2 and Victor B2 crews were trained in the missile's characteristics and operation. Navigators remained at Lindholme for a month, but pilots and air electronics officers spent only a week there before going to Gaydon for a further three-week course. The introduction of the missile meant a significant increase in work load, especially for the AEO, who had to monitor all the equipment in the Blue Steel Services Pack, located in the forward part of the bomb bay. On completing the ground course, crews would then undertake a short airborne conversion course, during which they would be screened by experienced Blue Steel crews before carrying out their own Blue Steel training sorties.

The operational version of Blue Steel was 35ft long, with a wing span of 13ft, and the maximum diameter of its body was 4ft 2¼in. Its range was 100 nautical miles, it could be launched from either high or low level, it attained a maximum speed of Mach 1.6 and it carried a thermonuclear warhead with a yield of approximately one megaton. It became fully operational in February 1963 with No 617 Squadron at RAF Scampton, somewhat later than planned, and subsequently equipped two more Vulcan squadrons

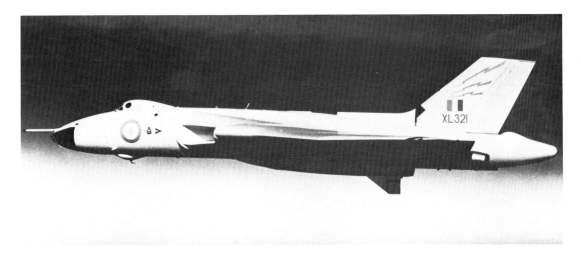

(Nos 27 and 83) and two Victor squadrons (Nos 100 and 139). Its importance lay in the fact that it gave the V-Force a continued operational viability into the mid-1960s in the face of increasingly sophisticated enemy fighter and SAM missile defences. In fact, it remained operational until 1970, after the RAF's strategic deterrent role had been taken over by the Royal Navy's Polaris-equipped nuclear-powered submarines.

As long ago as 1956, when Blue Steel was still in the early stages of development, the Air Staff had realised that the V-Force was going to need a stand-off weapon with a much greater range than 100nm, and a requirement had been issued for a long-range guided bomb which could fly for over 1,000nm at a height of 80,000ft and a speed of Mach 3. Studies had been made of a Mk 2 version of Blue Steel, which would have gone part of the way towards meeting this requirement, but in 1958 British enthusiasm was growing for an air-launched strategic ballistic missile system which would have more than met the Air Staff requirement, and which was then the subject of a United States Air Force design competition. Fifteen companies entered the running, and in May 1959 the Douglas Aircraft Corporation was named as prime contractor for the new weapon system.

Skybolt

The original designation of the weapon system for which Douglas received a design study contract in 1959 was WS-138A. On 5 February 1960, a further contract called for the building of research and development test vehicles, and the missile now began to take shape under the designation XGAM-87A, the name Skybolt being allocated to it. A two-stage, solid-fuel missile capable of hypersonic speeds (Mach 5) and ranges up to 1,150 miles, the 38ft long Skybolt ALBM (Air Launched Ballistic Missile) was to have altered the whole concept of strategic air warfare. Unlike a stand-off bomb such as Blue Steel, which was virtually a programmed extension of the bomber itself, Skybolt was a strategic delivery system in its own right, the function of the parent aircraft being simply to transport it to its launch point well outside the periphery of an enemy's defences. Skybolt itself came within the IRBM (Intermediate Range Ballistic Missile) category; in designing it, Douglas chose to sacrifice range and warhead size so that up to four missiles of this type could be carried on pylons under the wings of the Boeing B-52 or Convair B-58, each missile being individually targeted.

The British Government began to show an active interest in acquiring Skybolt for the RAF V-Force in 1959, and when in March the following year Prime Minister Harold Macmillan met President Dwight D. Eisenhower at Camp David a Memorandum of Agreement was concluded under which the missile would be supplied to the RAF. At this time, it was envisaged that Skybolt would be operational with Strategic Air Command by the end of 1963, to be carried by the powerful B-52H variant of the Stratofortress, the B-58B (the proposed Skybolt-carrying version of the Convair Hustler) having been cancelled.

The acquisition of Skybolt was held to be crucially important to the British nuclear deterrent, for on 13 April 1960 the British Minister of Defence, Mr Harold Watkinson, had announced in Parliament that Britain's own planned Intercontinental Ballistic Missile, the liquid-fuelled Blue Streak, was to be

cancelled as a military weapon and Skybolt ordered in its place. Since Britain could expect only a few minutes' warning of a hostile strike, liquid-fuelled missiles, with their time-consuming launch preparations, were no longer considered viable, and in any case 20 squadrons of American-built Thor IRBMs (three to a squadron) were already sited in East Anglia, these weapons having been loaned to the RAF in 1958. However, the Thor was also liquid-fuelled, and therefore its useful life would be limited. With the Thors expected to be phased out before the mid-1960s (they were, in fact, withdrawn in 1963) the British nuclear deterrent would devolve on a combination of Victor, Vulcan and Blue Steel. Skybolt appeared to offer the best means of maintaining the deterrent once Blue Steel's useful life was over, so the decision was taken to adopt it in preference to the other alternative, a small force of nuclear submarines armed with Polaris missiles.

On 12 January 1961, a B-52G made a six-hour flight carrying four dummy Skybolts. The first production model B-52H flew on 6 March and began aerodynamic flight compatibiity tests in June, but it was a B-52F (serial 57-038) which began flight trials with the weapon that autumn, dropping a series of inert rounds. On 29 January 1961, Vulcan B2 XH563

of No 83 Squadron arrived at the Douglas Company's test field at Santa Monica, California, to undergo electrical compatibility tests, and then went on for further trials to the Wright Air Development Division at Wright Patterson, AFB, Ohio.

Meanwhile, in the United Kingdom, Hawker Siddeley had been carrying out the modifications necessary to mate the missile with the Vulcan B2, and in July 1961 AEI were awarded a major contract for the production of the Vulcan/Skybolt interface equipment, which included an analog/digital converter. A British thermonuclear warhead was also being developed. In November 1961, Vulcan XH537 flew for the first time from the Weapons Research Division at Woodford with two dummy Skybolts on underwing pylons, and on 1 December this aircraft made the first dummy Skybolt drop. Three further drops were made, all with dummy rounds, by XH537 and XH538. These drops were made from 45,000ft at 0.84M.

During 1962 a British Joint Trials Force, eventually some 200 strong, was set up in the United States under the command of Wg Cdr Charles Ness at Eglin Air Force Base in Florida, home of the Skybolt trials teams, and joint development proceeded throughout the remainder of 1962 with Douglas and the USAF.

The first live launch of a Skybolt from a B-52 was made on 19 April 1962; unfortunately, although the first stage booster worked as planned, the second stage failed to ignite. There was further trouble during the second live launch on 29 June, when the first stage motor did not ignite correctly and the missile had to be destroyed by the range safety officers; and although both stages fired successfully at the third attempt, on 13 September, the missile veered off course and again had to be destroyed. Disappointing though these failures were, however, they were not unexpected in the development programme of what was a radical and extremely complex weapon, and on 25 September a fourth trial was made. On this occasion both stages fired, but the second only burned for 15sec. which meant that the Skybolt did not achieve its planned range of 900 miles.

Meanwhile, plans were being made to carry out live firings from a Vulcan early in 1963, and studies were in progress on the feasibility of adapting the Victor to carry two, four or even six Skybolts. It was consiered,

however, that the Victor was not so suitable as a carrier.

There was no reason to believe that Skybolt would be anything other than an extremely viable weapon in RAF service, or that it would fall much behind the target date for its debut with the Vulcan squadrons. Then came the blow: in December 1962, during talks at Nassau in the Bahamas, President John F. Kennedy informed Prime Minister Macmillan of his decision to cancel plans for the production of Skybolt. He offered to continue development of the missile on a jointly financed US-UK basis, but this offer was declined. An alternative suggestion – that the RAF should purchase Hound Dog air-breathing missiles, already proven and in service with SAC's B-52 force since 1960 – was also rejected on the grounds of technical difficulties. Another alternative, the provision of Polaris fleet ballistic missiles for which Britain would provide the warheads and the submarines, was accepted. But this spelt the end of RAF responsibility for the strategic nuclear deterrent role, which would be taken over by the Royal Navy.

The Nassau talks took place between 18 and 21 December 1962. The irony was that, while they were in progress, the B-52F trials aircraft took off from Eglin AFB on the 19th and launched a Skybolt over the Eastern Test Range; the missile worked perfectly and reached its target area, 1,000 miles away in the south Atlantic.

Left: A Skybolt ballistic missile seen here beneath a B-52G./*USAF*

Below: One of two AGN-28B Hound Dog air-to-ground weapons carried by B-52. This 1,200mph missile has a range of 500 miles. /*Boeing*

V–Force Operational Procedures

For RAF Bomber Command, the late 1950s – following the introduction of the Valiant in 1955 – were marked by a period of experiment and development, with the intermarriage of old and new operational techniques. Taking into account the Valiant's performance, which was a vast improvement over that of any previous RAF bomber, conventional bombing techniques remained basically similar to those in force since the latter part of World War 2, as the Suez operation had demonstrated; after 1956, however, the advent of nuclear weapons made greater demands on crews and aircraft, and accordingly a new set of operational procedures had to be devised.

A typical Valiant training sortie during this period would involve a 4-4½hr cross-country flight, with simulated radar bombing attacks against targets around the UK. The busiest crew members before such a sortie would be the navigators, the navigator (radar) assembling information on the assigned radar targets and the navigator (plotter) noting all relevant route information, including weather details. The co-pilot was responsible for all calculations involving such factors as loading, fuel, endurance and take-off and landing weights, while the air electronics officer collated all callsigns and classified codes which were to be used during the sortie. After each crew member had undergone his individual briefing, the crew would be assembled and briefed on the sortie by the captain. The aircraft would be handed over by the crew chief and its crew would enter the cockpit to carry out their pre-flight checks, which occupied about an hour in the case of a Valiant.

When a Valiant crew was called to readiness or summoned for an alert exercise, crew members reported to the Operations Wing (with sufficient kit for an indefinite stay away from base) and were briefed on the nature of the alert. Each crew would undergo the usual pre-flight briefing routine, and then all the crews would be subjected to further briefings by specialist officers; the AEOs would be briefed by the Wing AEO, for example. The crews would then go into a waiting posture while the aircraft was made combat ready, each Valiant having to meet a stringent preparation level. When this was achieved, crews would go out to their aircraft to carry out the appropriate checks; the cockpit door would then be locked and no-one allowed inside except crew members.

The crews would then await the alert call, which was sounded either by klaxon or station broadcast over the tannoy. The initial call brought them to 'Readiness One-Five' (15min) and they would remain inside the cockpit with the door locked and ground crew standing by, the aircraft crew connected by teletalk (known colloquially as the 'Bomber Box') to the Bomber Controller in the Bomber Command Operations Room. Over the teletalk, the crew could hear dispersal instructions being issued to other units; these usually followed a set pattern, with units being brought to five-minute readiness, followed by two-minute readiness, then scrambled. Engines were started at Readiness Zero Two; later, a simultaneous start technique was evolved, enabling all four engines to be started at the same time. After the order to scramble, squadron crews would either go straight into a training profile, a cross-country flight with radar bomb scores, or be dispersed to pre-determined airfields in clutches of four aircraft. Throughout its career, the V-Force relied on dispersal, ultimately to some 36 designated airfields, as security against surprised attack; unlike Strategic Air Command, it never maintained an airborne alert force. In the case of a prolonged exercise, lasting one or two weeks, the force would remain dispersed, the crews living alongside their aircraft and continually practising alert readiness checks with the Bomber Controller. A comprehensive debrief was held after each exercise, the results analysed and, if necessary, operational procedures amended.

As V-Force expertise grew, overseas exercises became more frequent. Squadrons would send detachments to Malaya (Exercise 'Sunflower') for up to a month, a series of local familiarisation flights being followed by a full-scale exercise with SEATO air forces. Squadron detachments were also made to Luqa, Malta (Exercise 'Sunspot'), during which crews would carry out visual bombing over the El Adem range, Libya, with 100lb practice and 1,000lb

Top right: A Valiant crew – two pilots, two navigators, AEO and crew chief – in typical RAF aircrew garb of the late 1950s.

Right: Aircrew of No 617 Squadron demonstrating a scramble to visiting German VIPs at Scampton on 21 November 1958./*RAF*

live HE bombs. There were also single-aircraft 'Lone Ranger' flights, mainly to El Adem, Cyprus and Nairobi; equivalent single-crew flights to Norway were known as 'Polar Bears' and those to the United States as 'Western Rangers'. The latter usually terminated at Offut Air Force Base, Omaha, Nebraska, the headquarters of Strategic Air Command.

All these exercises provided V-Force crews with invaluable operational training under widely differing conditions, as well as having the very worthwhile secondary effect of 'showing the flag' for the Royal Air Force. Further valuable training on a competitive basis was provided by the annual Bomber Command (later Strike Command) bombing competition, which introduced a considerable element of rivalry not only between individual crews, but also between the two RAF Bomber Groups – No 1 equipped with Vulcans and No 3 with Valiants (and Victor B1s from 1960). The competition would last for three days, with an optional fourth day to allow for bad weather. Each participating crew was accompanied by an umpire. The contest was very exacting, particularly for the navigators, who had to demonstrate their ability to operate using only limited equipment over a leg of about 800 miles. Astro-navigation featured prominently, the radar navigator taking celestial shots with a sextant and the navigator-plotter working out headings and ETAs with the information

so obtained. The leg terminated over a radar bombing site, the end-of-leg position being determined by a signal sent out from the aircraft. This was plotted on the ground and the navigation error calculated accordingly. AEOs were required to receive coded message groups within a specified time, and all the results achieved were collated to produce individual crew ratings.

The V-Force's viability as an effective strategic deterrent was constantly put to the test by war-situation exercises of varying intensity; for example those named 'Kinsman' meant dispersal, while 'Micky Finn' meant dispersal without notice. This was an annual exercise which involved other home-based commands of the RAF. In February 1962, the readiness state of the V-Force was further improved by the inauguration of the Bomber Command QRA (Quick Reaction Alert) plan, which initially involved one aircraft from each V-Force squadron being maintained in armed condition, at a later date on operational readiness platforms at the ends of runways, prepared to scramble at a moment's notice.

Below: Crews of No 207 Squadron (Valiants) debriefing at Malta following night attacks on Egyptian targets during the Suez operations of November 1956./*RAF*

Right: Valiant of No 214 Squadron being refuelled by a B(K)1./*RAF*

Below right: Valiant B1s on the ORP at Marham./*RAF*

By this time 'the deterrent' meant the Vulcans of No 1 Group and the Victors of No 3, for the bomber Valiants had now been assigned to the tactical role with NATO.

In 1962, with six years of experience behind it, the V-Force had become an extremely efficient organisation, with a strong nucleus of 'Select Star' crews – this being the highest V-Force crew classification, the others being 'Combat' and 'Select'. This expertise was embodied in and reflected by the QRA concept and in the ability of V-bombers to 'scramble' in 90sec. Crews were assigned to QRA on a one-a-week basis, plus one weekend in every three. For the most part, there was little to do except read and play cards, the crews living in their QRA caravans beside the 'Bomber Box', or at readiness in the cockpit depending on the alert state. In the latter case, once a scramble had been ordered all the pilot had to do was press the Mass Rapid Start Button and everything else happened automatically, the engines lighting up and the aircraft starting to move off the operational readiness platform, set an an angle to the runway, as thrust developed. The cockpits of both Vulcan and Victor were fitted with shields for protection against nuclear flash; only the forward vision panels were exposed during take-off and initial climb. During the remainder of the sortie the whole of the cockpit was blacked out, the route being flown by radar. The crew's task in this respect became more exacting when the V-Force went over to the low-level role, for the continual use of terrain-following radar required a high level of concentration on the part of the two pilots.

In the worst possible case, early warning radar would give the V-Force only four minutes' warning of an enemy missile attack. A more likely margin, even in the event of a surprise attack, would have been eight or perhaps even 15 minutes, and intelligence indications would probably have increased this margin still further to hours or even days.

Above: Vulcan B2 at RAF Goose Bay, Canada./*MoD*

Bottom: Valiants of the Marham Wing on the ORP./*RAF*

Right: Vulcan B2As of Nos 9 and 11 Squadrons at Waddington on QRA./*RAF*

Nevertheless, it was vital that a potential enemy should realise the impossibility of destroying the RAF's 'second-strike' capability on the ground; in other words, the RAF must be seen to demonstrate its quick reaction techniques regularly and efficiently. This it did with great skill and thoroughly, and only once in 10 years of maintaining the deterrent did it seem as though the V-Force might have to bring its striking power to bear in a real war situation. This was during the Cuban Missile Crisis of October 1962, when the V-Force was unobtrusively brought up to a high degree of readiness; civilian personnel on V-Force bases were sent home, the bases were sealed off from the outside and their perimeters secured by armed patrols, while the V-bombers were armed and

stood combat-ready for a period of three days. At no time during that period, however, was any part of the force ordered to scramble.

Training rounds of the Blue Steel ASM had been introduced into RAF service in the months before the Cuban Crisis, and since No 617 Squadron had achieved an emergency operational capability with

Below: Loading bombs into a No 9 Squadron Vulcan at Akrotiri during an exercise off Cyprus./*RAF*

Far right: XL512 a Victor K2 of No 57 Squadron at RAF Marham. /*A.P. Lovelock*

Bottom right: XA922, Victor B1, at Woodford awaiting tanker conversion./*P. Tomlin*

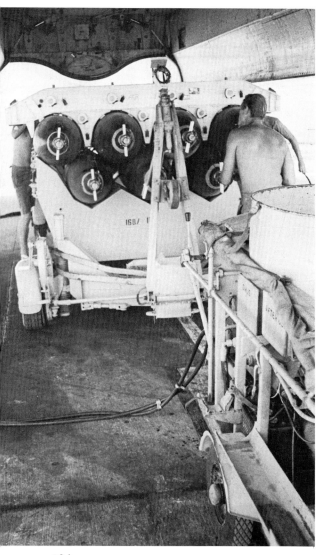

the weapon it would doubtless have been used had it proved necessary. The introduction of Blue Steel into full operational service the following year produced several variations in operational procedures, beginning with a complex fail-safe system. This meant that the weapon could only be launched after the first pilot, both the navigators and the AEO had each played his part in the pre-launch sequence. There were also strict safety precautions against contamination by the missile's hydrogen peroxide fuel, which could cause serious injury if it came into contact with human skin; for this reason a large water-filled bath was positioned near the aircraft during loading and unloading, so that anyone who did become contaminated could be immediately immersed. In the event of a missile malfunction while the weapon was still attached to the aircraft, the latter would fly to a pre-designated airfield where there was the necessary equipment to deal with such an emergency.

The introduction of low-level operations to the V-Force in 1964 led to an increase in overseas sorties, as low-level training in the UK was restricted by the density of urban areas and air traffic. Goose Bay in Labrador, where a small Royal Air Force detachment was already located to service and despatch 'Western Ranger' aircraft on their flights to and from Offutt AFB, was selected as a suitable base, and every week throughout the year crews of the medium bomber force crossed the Atlantic to fly three or four low-level sorties during an eight-day period over some of the wildest territory in the world, and certainly some of the most difficult from the radar navigation point of view.

No survey of V-Force training, however short, would be complete without mention of the Bomber Command Development Unit, which was responsible for the modification and evaluation of equipment and also for recommending tactics and operational procedures. Formed at Wittering in May 1954 and initially equipped with Canberras, it received its first V-Bombers – three Valiants of No 138 Squadron, complete with air and ground crews – in June 1959, and the following March it moved to Finningley. At a late date, Vulcans also joined the BCDU Trials Flight, and squadron aircraft were attached to it from time to time. The unit's work covered the whole spectrum of V-Force operations, much of the task involving trials with radio, radar and ECM equipment, and the development of tactics and techniques in navigation, bombing and ECM operation. The unit also carried out trials on parachutes, survival packs, instruments, landing systems and aids, fuelling, braking parachutes, engine mass rapid start techniques and camouflage methods, as well as a lot of other work which remains

highly classified. The BCDU retained a great deal of autonomy, working closely with establishments such as the A&AEE Boscombe Down, the RAE Farnborough, RRE Malvern and the CFE, as well as with the various aircraft and component manufacturers. The contribution it made over the years to V-Force efficiency was of inestimable value.

On 30 April 1968, Bomber and Fighter Commands merged to form RAF Strike Command. Fourteen months later, on 30 June 1969, the RAF's QRA strategic nuclear deterrent role was handed over to the Polaris submarines of the Royal Navy. For seven years, ever since the inauguration of QRA, the RAF had maintained the highest state of combat readiness it had ever known in peacetime, and it should not be forgotten that, in the event of a nuclear war, it would probably have been the V-Force that would have carried out the first manned strategic strike on the enemy's defences, preceding the B-52s of Strategic Air Command. In the words of Air Chief Marshal Sir John Grandy, the Chief of the Air Staff when the V-Force relinquished its QRA role:

'. . . The way in which QRA has been performed and the reaction of the force to the operational demands of our plans and those of SACEUR has been an unsurpassed demonstration of professional skill, dedication and tenacity. The long hours of arduous duty in cockpits, crew rooms, dispersal, hangars and operations rooms have brought the reward of knowing that a vital task has been successfully completed.'

Although the role for which they were originally intended has been relinquished for more than a decade at the time of writing, the V-bombers are still very much in evidence. The Scampton Wing comprises the Vulcan B2s of Nos 35 and 617 Squadrons, as well as those of No 230 Operational Conversion Unit and the SR2s of No 27 Squadron, while RAF Waddington is shared by the Vulcans of Nos 9, 44, 50 and 101 Squadrons, all assigned to the tactical role. They will be progressively phased out from 1982, when the squadrons begin to re-equip with the Tornado, but the SR2s of No 27 Squadron will still be flying for some time after that. So will the Victor K2s of the RAF Tanker Wing, which are scheduled to be joined in their role by a number of converted VC10s.

It seems, therefore, that the characteristic delta and crescent wing shapes, synonymous for so long with the spearhead of the RAF's nuclear deterrent power, will be a familiar sight in the skies of Europe and beyond throughout the 1980s.

VALIANT

EQUIPMENT LAYOUT

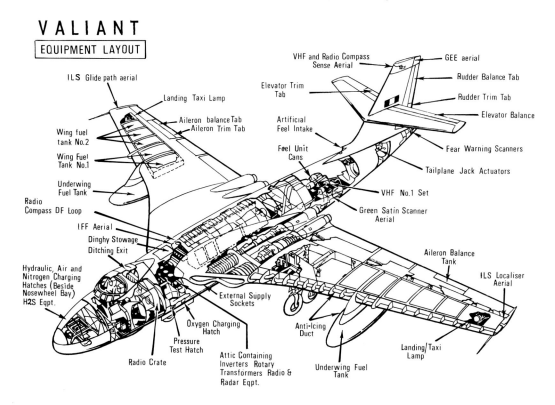

Appendices

1 The V-Bombers: Main Data

Vickers Valiant B Mk 1
Length: 108ft 3in
Span: 114ft 4in
Weight: 75,880lb (empty)
175,000lb (max loaded)
Crew: Five
Max speed: 0.82M (290kts) at 40,000ft
Service ceiling: 49,000ft
Range: (10,000lb bomb load halfway) 3,450 miles without reserves, 4,500 miles with underwing tanks.
Weapons: One 10,000lb MC Mk 1 nuclear store, or tactical nuclear stores, or 21 1,000lb conventional bombs.
Engines: Four 10,000lb st Rolls-Royce Avon 204/205.
Other Data: Internal equipment included Gee H Mk II, IFF, T4 bombsight, 'Green Satin' doppler navigation system, Rebecca Mk 10, Eureka Mk 10 and tail warning radar

Avro (Hawker Siddeley) Vulcan	B Mk 1 variants	B Mk 2 variants
Length:	97ft 1in	99ft 11in
Span:	99ft 0in	111ft 0in
Weight loaded:	170,000lb	200,000lb
Crew:	Five	Five
Max speed: (40,000ft)	0.86M	0.9M
Service ceiling:	55,000ft	60,000ft
Range:	3,000ft	4,600 miles (high level)
Weapons:	Free-falling nuclear stores or 21 1,000lb conventional bombs	As for B1, or one Avro Blue Steel ASM
Engines:	Four Bristol Olympus 101, 102 or 104 engines of up to 13,500lb st	Four Bristol Olympus 200, 201 or 301 engines of up to 20,000lb st

Handley Page Victor	B Mk 1 variants	B Mk 2 variants
Length:	114ft 11in	114ft 11in
Span:	110ft	120ft
Weight loaded:	180,000lb	223,000lb
Crew:	Five	Five
Max speed: (40,000ft)	0.9M	0.95M
Service ceiling:	55,000ft	60,000ft
Range:	2,500 miles	3,500 miles
Weapons:	Nuclear stores or 35 1,000lb conventional bombs	As for B1, or one Blue Steel ASM
Engines:	Four 11,050lb st AS Sapphire 202/207	Four RR Conway RCo11/17 Mk 201 of up to 20,600lb st

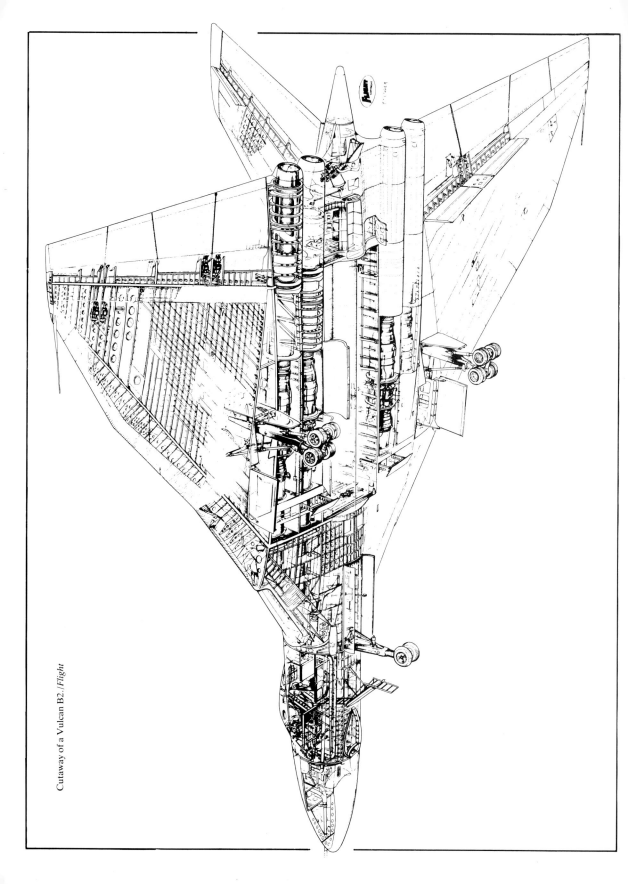

Cutaway of a Vulcan B2. /*Flight*

Cutaway of a Victor B Mk 2./*Flight*

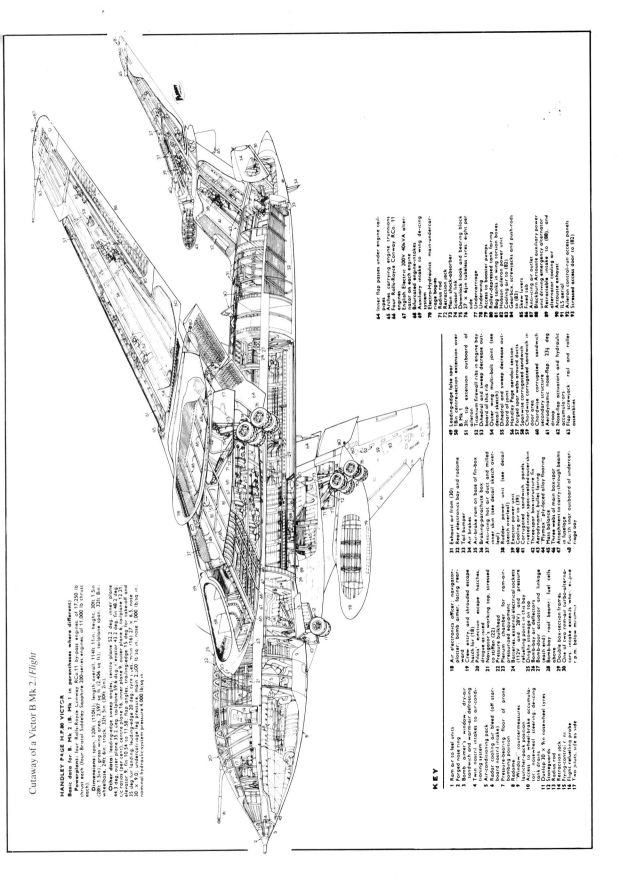

HANDLEY PAGE H.P.80 VICTOR

Basic data for B. Mk 2 (B. Mk 1 in parentheses where different)

Powerplant: four Rolls-Royce Conway RCo.11 by-pass engines, of 17,250 lb thrust each (four Bristol Siddeley Sapphire 200-series engines, of 11,000 lb thrust each).

Dimensions: span, 120ft (110ft); length overall, 114ft 11in; height, 30ft 1.5in (28ft 1.5in); gross wing area, 2,597 sq ft (2,406 sq ft); tailplane span, 32ft 8in; wheelbase, 24ft 6in; track, 32ft (30ft 2in).

Other data: leading-edge sweep angles, centre plane 52.2 deg, inner plane 44.3 deg, outer plane 35.2 deg; tailplane 59.6 deg / elevator 43.2 deg, fin 48.2 deg; (c ratios (per cent), centre plane 16, inner plane 9, outer plane 6, tailplane 12.1, elevator 9.6, fin 10.54 to 11.58; flap angles, trailing-edge 15 deg, take-off and 35 deg for landing, leading-edge 20 deg; tyre pressures, main 2,500 lb/sq in, nose 1,000 lb/sq in, nominal hydraulic-system pressure 4,000 lb/sq in.

KEY

1 Ram air to feel units
2 Forged nose ring
3 Bomb aimer's window dry-air sandwich and warm-air defrosting
4 Twin nostril air-intakes to air-conditioning system
5 Air-conditioning pack
6 Radar cooling air bleed (off starboard nostril intake)
7 Pressure bulkhead for prone bombing position
8 Radome
9 "Window" countermeasures launcher-pack position
10 Access to wheel-brake accumulator, nosewheel steering, de-icing tank drains
11 Dunlop 30 × 9in nose-wheel tyres
12 Stoneguards
13 Radius rod
14 Retraction rack
15 Flying-control runs
16 Flight refuelling probe
17 Two pilots, side by side
18 Air electronics officer, navigator-plotter; bomb aimer, facing rearward
19 Crew entry, and shrouded escape hatch for (18)
20 Pilots' ejection escape hatches, drogue-actuated
21 Navigator's working top, stressed to stiffen (22)
22 Pressure bulkhead
23 Plenum chamber for ram-air pressurized equipment
24 Batteries, external electrical sockets (112V and 28V) and pressure refuelling point in this bay
25 Dinghy stowage on top
26 Bomb-bay air deflectors
27 Bomb-door actuator and linkage (each end)
28 Bomb-bay roof beams: fuel cells above
29 Double box-section frames
30 One of two ram-air turbo-alternators; intake extends when engine r.p.m. below minimum
31 Exhaust air from (30)
32 Rear electronics bay and radome
33 Tail bumper
34 Air-brake
35 Air-brake run on base of fin-box
36 Braking-parachute box
37 Anti-icing hot air duct and milled inner skin (see detail sketch overleaf)
38 Rudder power unit (see detail sketch overleaf)
39 Elevator power unit
40 Cooling air to (39)
41 Corrugated sandwich panels, riveted-inner, spot-welded outer-skin
42 Three-spar box-structure fin
43 Anti-drag bullet fairing
44 "Plymax" ply-faced alloy flooring
45 Mass balance
46 Nose-flap actuators and hydraulic accumulators
47 Attachment to carry-through beams in fuselage
48 Fourth spar outboard of undercarriage bay
49 Leading-edge false spar
50 18in centre-section extension over aileron
51 3ft tip extension outboard of aileron
52 Titanium firewall ribs in engine bay
53 Dihedral and sweep decrease outboard of this rib
54 Outer wing multi-bolt joint (see detail sketch)
55 Dihedral and sweep decrease outboard of joint
56 Handley Page aerofoil section
57 Forged spar webs around ducts
58 Spanwise corrugated sandwich
59 Chordwise corrugated sandwich in secondary structure
60 Chordwise corrugated sandwich
61 Aerodynamic nose-flap, 23½ deg droop
62 Nose-flap actuators and hydraulic accumulators
63 Flap screwjack rail and roller assemblies
64 Inner flap passes under engine tail-pipes
65 Arches carrying engine trunnions
66 Four Rolls-Royce Conway RCo.11
67 English Electric 200V 40kVA alternator on each engine
68 Bifurcated engine-intakes
69 Auxiliary intake to wing de-icing system
70 Electro-Hydraulics main-undercarriage bogies
71 Radius rod
72 Retraction jack
73 Main shock-absorber
74 Scissor-link
75 Downlock hook and bearing block
76 27 × 6in tubeless tyres, eight per side
77 Undercarriage
78 Underwing
79 Access to booster pumps
80 Roller-depressed tank fairing
81 Bag-tanks in wing (crison boxes
82 Hobson aileron power unit
83 Cooling air to (82)
84 Gearbox, aerofoil section
85 Skew levers
86 Fixed tab
87 Anti-icing air outlet
88 Blackburn Artouste auxiliary power unit driving emergency alternator
89 Retractable intake to (88), and alternator cooling
90 Artouste exhaust
91 ILS aerial
92 Aileron control-run access panels to (82)
93 Stressed access door to (82)

2 The V-Force Squadrons

No 7 Squadron

Formerly an Avro Lincoln squadron which had disbanded early in 1956, No 7 re-formed as part of the Medium Bomber Force with Valiant B1s at Honington on 1 November that year. The squadron disbanded again in October 1962, but later re-formed as a Canberra unit with a special ECM role. Operational 1980. Representative Valiant aircraft: WP207, WZ381, XD826.

No 9 Squadron

This squadron re-formed with Vulcan B2s in March 1962 at Coningsby, having disbanded as a Canberra squadron in July 1961. It later moved to Cottesmore and early in 1969 left this location for Akrotiri in Cyprus, where it formed the Near East Bomber Wing together with No 35 Squadron. It returned to the UK in February 1975 to becme part of the Waddington Wing, and was operational in 1980. Representative aircraft: XH536, XL386, XM600.

No 10 Squadron

Re-formed on 15 April 1958, having previously operated Canberras, No 10 was the first squadron to receive the Victor B1, and was based at RAF Cottesmore. It disbanded in February 1964, re-forming on 1 July 1966 as a VC10 squadron at RAF Brize Norton. Operational 1980. Representative Victor B1 aircraft: XA928, XA936, XA939.

No 12 Squadron

Originally one of the three squadrons of the Coningsby Wing in No 1 Group, No 12 re-formed at that location in July 1962 with Vulcan B2s. It moved to Cottesmore with Nos 9 and 35 Squadrons at the end of 1964, and disbanded on 31 December 1967. It

later re-formed with Buccaneer S2Bs and was operational in 1980. Representative Vulcan B2 aircraft: XH560, XM597, XM602.

No 15 Squadron

The second Victor squadron, No 15 formed alongside No 10 at Cottesmore on 1 September 1958 and remained part of No 3 Group until October 1964, when it disbanded. It re-formed on 1 October 1970 as a Buccaneer S2B unit, and was operational at Laarbruch in Germany in 1980. Representative Victor B1 aircraft: XA925, XH613, XH651.

No 18 Squadron

In July 1957, No 199 Squadron received its first Valiant aircraft at Honington, and its identity was changed to No 18 Squadron with a move to RAF Finningley on 16 December 1968. The squadron operated a mixture of Canberras and Valiants (six of the latter) in an ECM role, disbanding on 31 March 1963. It re-formed in January the following year as a Wessex heliopter squadron in No 38 Group. Representative Valiants: WP211, WP213, WZ372.

No 27 Squadron

The second squadron to equip with the Vulcan B2, No 27 re-formed as part of the Scampton Wing alongside No 83 on 1 April 1961, and in 1963 it became operational with the Blue Steel air to surface missile. The squadron disbanded in March 1972, re-forming on 1 November 1973 in the maritime radar reconnaissance role with Vulcan SR2s at Scampton. Operational 1980. Representative aircraft: XH555, XJ823, XL444.

No 35 Squadron

Re-formed in December 1962, with Vulcan B2s, No 35 became the third squadron of the Coningsby Wing, alongside Nos 9 and 12. Early in 1969 it left for Akrotiri, Cyprus, with No 9 to form the Near East Air Force Bomber Wing, returning to the UK in February 1975. It was operational in 1980 as part of the Scampton Wing. Representative aircraft: XM604, XH562, XJ781.

No 44 (Rhodesia) Squadron

Re-formed at RAF Waddington in August 1960, No 44 initially received the eight Vulcan B1s which had belonged to No 83 Squadron, the latter having re-equipped with B2s. The B1s were progressively converted to B1A standard, the first – XA904 – returning to the squadron in January 1961. It re-equipped with the Vulcan B2 in January 1968, and was operational as part of the Waddington Wing in 1980. Representative aircraft: XA896, XA904, XM599.

No 49 Squadron

A former Lincoln bomber unit, No 49 Squadron re-formed with Valiants at Wittering in May 1956 and was later heavily involved in nuclear weapons trials, one of its Valiants (WZ366, Sqn Ldr Flavell) making the first air drop of a British nuclear weapon on 11 October 1956 and another (ZD818, Wg Cdr Hubbard) dropping the first British H-Bomb on 15 May 1957. During 1960-61 No 49 was one of three Valiant squadrons assigned to the tactical role under SACEUR; it was disbanded on 1 May 1965, following the withdrawal of the Valiant from service. Representative aircraft: XD818, WZ366, XD824.

No 50 Squadron

Re-formed at Waddington on 1 August 1961, No 50 Squadron received four Vulcan B1s and five B1As which had previously belonged to No 617. The squadron re-equipped with the Vulcan B2 from January 1968 and was still operational as part of the Waddington Wing in 1980. Representative aircraft: XH482, XA909, XH506.

No 55 Squadron

One of No 3 Group's Victor squadrons, No 55 re-formed at Honington in September 1960 and was initially equipped with Victor B1s, later receiving the B1A. In May 1965 it became the first unit to equip with the Victor B(K)1A two-point tanker and subsequently moved to Marham, where it received three-point tankers in January 1967. On 1 July 1975 the squadron became the first to equip with the more powerful Victor K2, and was still operational with these aircraft in 1980. Representative aircraft: XH588, XH614, XH646.

No 57 Squadron

Re-formed at Honington on 1 January 1959, this squadron was equipped with Victor B1s and later 1As and its career closely matched that of No 55. In January 1966 it moved to Marham where it equipped with Victor K1/1A tankers, and on 7 June 1976 it received the first of its Victor K2s, with which it was still operational in 1980. Both Nos 55 and 57 Squadrons, while based at Honington, were deployed to Singapore during the Indonesian Confrontation of 1963. Representative aircraft: XA926, XH649, XH620.

No 83 Squadron

The RAF's first Vulcan squadron, No 83 re-formed at Waddington in May 1957, receiving the first of its Vulcan B1s (XA905) on 11 July. Nine more aircraft were received by the end of September. No 83 later became the first squadron to become fully operational with the Vulcan B2 in December 1960, having moved to Scampton in October. In 1963, No 83 was the second Vulcan squadron to become operational with Blue Steel. The squadron disbanded in 1969. Representative aircraft: XA901, XH480, XJ781.

No 90 Squadron

The second of the Honington Valiant squadrons, No 90 joined No 7 there in January 1957. From 1 October 1961 it became part of the tanker force at Marham with Valiant BK1s, and disbanded early in 1965. Representative aircraft: WP223, WZ377, ZD871.

No 100 Squadron

Re-formed on 1 May 1962, No 100 Squadron was the second of the two Victor squadrons at RAF Wittering, the other being No 139, and its B2s were later adapted to carry Blue Steel, the squadron becoming operational with this weapon in January 1964. The squadron disbanded on 1 October 1968, later re-forming with Canberras in the target facilities role. Operational at Marham 1980. Representative aircraft: XL160, XM715, XM717.

No 101 Squadron

Re-formed at RAF Finningley on 15 October 1957, No 101 was the second front-line unit to operate the Vulcan B1. In June 1961 the squadron moved to Waddington with five B1s and two B1As, re-equipping with the B2 in January 1968. No 101 Squadron was operational as part of the Waddington Wing in 1980. Representative aircraft: XA909, XH532, XM609.

No 138 Squadron

The first squadron to receive the Vickers Valiant, No 138 received its first aircraft (WP206) in February 1955 at Gaydon, moving to Wittering with six aircraft the following July. In October 1956 the squadron detached to Malta to take part in the Suez operations. It disbanded in April 1962. Representative aircraft: WP203, WZ400, XD866.

No 139 (Jamaica) Squadron

The first Victor B2 Squadron, No 139 formed at Wittering on 1 February 1962 with an initial strength of six aircraft. In 1963 it re-equipped with Victor B2Rs, modified to carry Blue Steel. The squadron disbanded on 31 December 1968. Representative aircraft: XL190, XH673, XL513.

No 148 Squadron

Formed at Marham in July 1956, No 148 was one of the Valiant squadrons which took part in the Suez operation that autumn, one of its aircraft (XD815) becoming the first V-bomber to drop bombs in anger. In 1961 No 148 became one of the three Valiant squadrons assigned to NATO in the tactical role. It was disbanded on 28 April 1965. Representative aircraft: XD814, WZ379, XD858.

No 199 Squadron

One of the most experienced electronic countermeasures units in the Royal Air Force, No 199 Squadron had only a short career as part of the V-Force, receiving Valiants at Honington in July 1957 and changing its identity to No 18 Squadron with a move to RAF Finningley on 16 December 1958. Representative aircraft: WP213, WP216, WZ372.

No 207 Squadron

Having previously operated Boeing Washingtons, No 207 Squadron re-formed at Marham in May 1956 with an establishment for eight Valiants, and in October had six aircraft in Malta for air operations against Egypt. In 1960 it was assigned to SACEUR in the tactical role, and was disbanded on 1 May 1965 following the withdrawal of the Valiant from service. Representative aircraft: WP219, WP221, XD873.

No 214 Squadron

Re-formed at Marham as a Valiant squadron in the Medium Bomber Force in March 1956, No 214 took part in the operations against Egypt later that year. In March 1958 the squadron undertook operational flight refuelling trials and subsequently became the RAF's first tanker squadron, pioneering many refuelling techniques. After a short disbandment following the withdrawal of the Valiants, No 214 re-formed once more on 1 July 1966 at Marham with Victor B(K)1s, continuing in the tanker role until its final disbandment on 28 January 1977. Representative aircraft: WZ379, XD812, XD858 (Valiant); XA927, XA930, XH667 (Victor).

No 543 Squadron

Forming at Gaydon on 1 June 1955 in the strategic reconnaissance role, No 543 Squadron was the second unit to receive Valiants B(PR)1s. It subsequently moved to Wyton, where it remained throughout its career. Folllowing the premature retirement of the Valiant in January 1965 the squadron changed to Victors, receiving its first SR 2 on 18 May 1965 and its last on 21 June 1966. No 543 Squadron disbanded on 24 May 1974. Representative aircraft: XL230, XM715, XM716.

No 617 Squadron

Famous as the wartime 'Dam Busters', No 617 Squadron re-formed at Scampton on 1 May 1958 with Vulcan B1s, and in November 1960 received the first B1A conversion, XH505. From September 1961 the squadron re-equipped with Vulcan B2s, and in February 1963 it was the first to reach fully operational status with the Blue Steel missile. On the withdrawal of Blue Steel No 617 reverted to the free-fall bombing role, and was still operational as part of the Scampton Wing in 1980. Representative aircraft: XH482, XL317, XH503.

No 230 Operational Conversion Unit

Re-formed at Waddington in August 1956 as the Vulcan OCU, No 230 received its first Vulcans, XA895 and XA898, in January 1957, and by May that year it had seven Vulcan B1s on charge. In July 1960 it received its first Vulcan B2, XH558, and began to relinquish its B1/1As in 1964, so that by the end of 1965 the OCU was equipped solely with B2s. In 1980 the OCU was still operational at Scampton, its task still conversion to and standardisation on the Vulcan B2/2A.

No 232 Operational Conversion Unit

Formed at Gaydon in June 1955, No 232 OCU's original task was to train Valiant crews and also to carry out intensive flying trials with the new V-bomber. The first OCU course went to form No 138 Squadron. On 28 November 1957 the OCU received its first Victor B1, XA931, and until 1964 was responsible for training all Valiant and Victor crews. With the demise of the Valiant it then became an all-Victor OCU, and in September 1961 it assumed the responsibility for Victor B2 trials at Cottesmore. The Tanker Training Flight at Marham was re-designated 232 OCU in February 1970, and in 1980 the OCU was still responsible for training and standardisation of Victor K2 tanker crews.